Entrepreneur MAGAZINE'S POCKET GUIDES

Mortgages and Refinancing

GET THE BEST RATES

Entrepreneur Press and
Jason R. Rich

EP
Entrepreneur. Press

Editorial Director: Jere L. Calmes
Cover Design: Beth Hansen-Winter
Editorial and Production Services: CWL Publishing Enterprises, Inc.,
Madison, WI, www.cwlpub.com

This publication is designed to provide accurate and authoritative information in regard to the subject matter covered. It is sold with the understanding that the publisher is not engaged in rendering legal, accounting or
other professional services. If legal advice or other expert assistance is
required, the services of a competent professional person should be sought.

Library of Congress Cataloging-in-Publication Data

Rich, Jason.
   Mortgages and refinancing : get the best rates / by Entrepreneur Press
and Jason R. Rich.
     p. cm. — (Entrepreneur pocket guides)
  ISBN 1-59918-039-1 (alk. paper)
  1. Mortgage loans. 2. Mortgage loans—Refinancing. I. Entrepreneur
Press. II. Title.
HG2040.15.R53 2006
332.7'22—dc22

                2006020659

12 11 10 09 08 07 06   10 9 8 7 6 5 4 3 2 1

Contents

Introduction

Homeownership has many financial benefits, plus potential perks in terms of the lifestyle you can achieve. After all, homeownership is a huge part of the American dream! By owning your own home, you're acquiring a significant asset (which will hopefully go up in value), which adds to your net worth.

Since most people don't have the cash on hand to pay for their home outright, they typically acquire a mortgage to finance their purchase. During the ten, 15, 20, or 30 years they're paying off their mortgage, many homeowners opt to refinance that mortgage, for a variety of reasons, such as to cut their monthly payment by reducing their interest rate. Also, as they're paying down their mortgage or after they've paid it off, they can tap the equity they've built up in their home for a wide range of purposes.

Mortgages and Refinancing: Get the Best Rates is an easy-to-understand introduction to obtaining a mortgage, refinancing, and using the equity you have in your home.

This book will explain what a mortgage is, describe some of the many of different mortgage products available to you, walk you through the process of applying for a mortgage and getting your application approved, and provide countless tips and strategies to save you money and time.

MORTGAGE *Mortgage*–A mortgage is a loan for which the home is used as collateral. If the borrower fails to make the monthly pay-**TERMS** ments on the mortgage, the lender could foreclose on the property. Traditionally, a mortgage was available from a bank, credit union, or savings and loan, and it had a fixed interested rate for 15, 20, 25, or 30 years. This was called a *fixed-rate mortgage*. To quality, a borrower needed to have a high credit score, be employed, have enough money to make a down payment of 20 percent of the property's sale price, and meet other criteria. Today, there are literally hundreds of mortgage products available and the qualification requirements are dramatically different (in many cases less stringent) from mortgages decades ago. This makes it possible for more people to get approved for mortgages and become homeowners.

If you already have a mortgage, this book will introduce you to the concept of refinancing your loan, discuss the pros and cons of refinancing, and explain the many options available to you. You'll also discover many reasons why people refinance their homes to save money, obtain cash, pay off debts, renovate their homes, or somehow improve their lifestyle by tapping into the equity they've built up in their property.

MORTGAGE TERMS

Refinance (aka refi)—The process of refinancing involves applying for a new mortgage to replace your current one. The goal of refinancing is typically to obtain a lower interest rate, reduce the monthly payment, reduce the duration of the loan, or cash out some of the equity in the home. There are many reasons why it might be advantageous to refinance. By refinancing, you can change the type of mortgage product you possess and go, for example, from a fixed-rate mortgage to a variable-rate mortgage or an interest-only mortgage. You can also stay with a fixed-rate mortgage, but change the terms of the loan. When you refinance, you can stay with your current lender or apply for a new mortgage with another lender, who may offer more favorable terms.

While this book certainly won't make you a real estate or mortgage expert, it will provide you with the insight and information you need to find a qualified mortgage broker or lender to help you with each step of the home-financing or refinancing process, plus give you the core knowledge you need to ensure that you make the best financial decisions for your unique situation.

Throughout this book, pay attention to the tips, warnings, and terms that are highlighted. These provide quick pieces of helpful advice or information that are extremely important. Also, be sure to use the dozens of additional resources described throughout this book and reference the Glossary found at the end of the book. These resources will help you save time and money, avoid unnecessary complications and hassles, and gain additional knowledge. Later in this book, you'll read detailed interviews with home financing and real estate professionals who will provide their personal advice, tips, and insight into what it takes to become a homeowner or refinance a mortgage.

One of the most important steps to qualifying, applying, and ultimately getting approved for the right type of mortgage is to work with a knowledgeable, experienced, and highly reputable lender or mortgage broker. It's vital that you find someone who will invest the necessary time to ensure that you obtain the right information and appropriate type of financing/mortgage to meet your unique needs. This book covers finding the best lender or mortgage broker to work with and then negotiating the best rates.

Mortgages and Refinancing: Get the Best Rates

*Mortgage broker–*This is an intermediary between the borrower and the lender. Most mortgage brokers represent multiple lenders and will work to find a lender that's most apt to approve your application based on your unique financial and credit situation. Mortgage brokers can typically offer a broader range of mortgage products than a traditional bank. It's important to understand, however, that a mortgage broker, although working to land your business, is not obligated to give you the best rates. It's your responsibility to shop around, determine what you should be able to qualify for, and then negotiate with the broker. Mortgage brokers earn a fee and/or commission for their services. These fees may be separate from the fees the lender charges. When shopping around, ask how each mortgage broker is compensated and consider those fees. Negotiate with the mortgage broker to obtain the lowest possible fees and interest rate.

Over 80 percent of the homebuyers in the U.S. work through a mortgage broker. As of 2005, there were over 20,000 mortgage brokerage companies in America.

*Correspondent lender–*In addition to mortgage brokers and direct lenders, you'll also find hybrid companies that offer borrowers the benefits of working with a direct lender and the flexibility of working with a broker who represents many mortgage products. A correspondent lender makes approval decisions and initially funds the loan, as a mortgage banker or direct lender would. Upon closing the loan, however, the correspondent lender then sells the loan to another lender for servicing. As the borrower, you'll be dealing with the banker who will be funding your loan right from the start, yet who will be able to shop your mortgage around to find you the best rates and terms. Typically, a correspondent lender will offer more competitive rates than ordinary brokers. When shopping around for a broker or lender, ask if the company is a correspondent lender.

Who Are Today's Homeowners?

In the past, homeownership was reserved for middle- to high-income people with steady, well-paying jobs, excellent credit, money for a down payment, and the ability to qualify for a 15-, 20-, or 30-year fixed-rate mortgage from their local bank or other financial institution. Today, there are so many mortgage and financing options available that the old requirements simply no longer apply.

Today's homeowners are single professionals, newlyweds, families, single parents with kids, and retired people who were able to qualify for some type of mortgage. Unlike in the past, even people with poor credit or little or no money for a down payment can often qualify for some type of home financing. In fact, thanks to no-income-verification mortgages, interest-only mortgages, adjustable-rate mortgages, fixed-rate mortgages, balloon mortgages, and countless other financing options, more people than ever can qualify for some type of home financing, allowing them to stop throwing away money on monthly rent and begin to truly enjoy the financial and lifestyle perks of homeownership.

Mortgages and Refinancing: Get the Best Rates is all about helping ordinary people figure out whether or not they can qualify for some type of home financing in order to purchase a home. The book also focuses on refinancing, second mortgages, and home equity loans.

Here are some of the topics you'll find in this book:

- An introduction to mortgages and refinancing (Chapter 1)
- Determining if you qualify for a mortgage (Chapter 2)
- Choosing the right mortgage broker or lender (Chapter 3)
- The mortgage prequalification process (Chapter 4)
- Choosing the best type of mortgage to apply for (Chapter 5)
- An introduction to refinancing (Chapter 6)
- The pros and cons of second mortgages and home equity loans (Chapter 7)
- The closing (Chapter 8)

While this book covers the basics on how to determine the best type of mortgage to apply for, how to get prequalified, and how to apply for a mortgage, for example, it's not meant to be a comprehensive resource that'll teach you everything about mortgages. Instead, you'll learn the core information you'll definitely need. You'll then be provided with tips and strategies for finding a reputable and knowledgeable mortgage broker or lender who will be able to help you choose the best financing options for your individual situation.

Many people in America could qualify for a mortgage and become homeowners, but they don't realize it. This is often because they don't have excellent credit, a way to gather enough money for a 20-percent down payment, or employment for which they can document a steady income. Many people simply don't know enough about the home-buying process to even think becoming homeowners is a possibility. Well, chances are, if you have a steady job and you've managed to pay your rent and support yourself and your family, there's probably a way for you to become a homeowner in the not-so-distant future.

Many people who currently have a mortgage don't realize that they could potentially cut their monthly payment, reduce the time it'll take to pay off the mortgage, or use the equity they've build up in their home by refinancing. People in need of extra cash could tap the equity they have in their homes by obtaining a second mortgage or a home equity loan or line of credit. Never before have so many home financing options been available to such a broad range of people.

Common Misconceptions About Homeownership

One of the biggest reasons why people don't consider homeownership is because they believe one or more of the common misconceptions about buying a home. Many people are under the misguided impression that homeownership isn't within their reach. These people continue to believe that the requirements that applied 10, 20, or 30 years ago still apply today.

These common misconceptions include the following:

- You must have excellent credit (a credit score in the high 700s or better) to qualify for a mortgage.
- You must have a full-time, steady job and earn enough money to fall into the upper-middle or upper income bracket.
- You need to have enough money in savings to pay at least 20 percent down.
- The month-to-month cost of homeownership is much higher than renting.
- Becoming a homeowner is too much of a responsibility and commitment.

If you haven't considered homeownership because you've believed one or more of these misconceptions, it's time to re-evaluate your situation and take active steps to determine if you could qualify for one of the many types of mortgage products available now that weren't available 10, 20, or 30 years ago. If you earn a steady income, have at least average credit (meaning a credit score over 620), and are able to afford your monthly rent, chances are you could qualify for some type of mortgage and become a homeowner.

Likewise, if you already have a mortgage, but you're under the impression you're locked into the terms of that loan for the next 10, 20, or 30 years, this too is incorrect, especially if your financial situation, credit score, and/or employment situation have improved since you acquired your mortgage.

MORTGAGE **Throughout this book, the term** *mortgage products* refers to the many types of mortgages available from mortgage
HELP brokers and various types of lenders (banks, credit unions, savings and loans, mortgage companies, investors, the government, etc.). For example, a 15-year fixed-rate mortgage and a 30-year adjustable-rate mortgage are mortgage products.

There are dozens of types of mortgages available from literally thousands of lenders. Hopefully, by reading this book you will discover that homeownership is within your reach or, if you have a mortgage, that refinancing could save you a fortune. You may discover, however, that at this time you don't

---

☆ ☆ WARNING ☆ ☆

Unfortunately, not everyone will immediately qualify for some type of home financing and be able to buy a home after reading this book. If you don't qualify for a mortgage at present, this book will advise you on actions you can take to meet mortgage approval requirements in the future. This might mean paying off debts, taking steps to boost your credit score, being able to show a longer employment history, saving up more money for a down payment, or having inaccurate information removed from your credit report.

---

yet qualify for the financing you'll need. This book will help you make this determination and plan your future accordingly.

If you're a first-time home buyer, seriously consider reading, in addition to this book, *Why Rent? Own Your Dream Home!* (another book in the Entrepreneur Pocket Guides series written by Jason R. Rich), because it walks you through the entire home-buying process, including providing information about mortgages and financing.

The goal of *Mortgages and Refinancing: Get the Best Rates* is to help potential or current homeowners get the best rates possible when applying for any type of mortgage and then best use the equity they've built in their homes. If this is information of interest to you, read on!

—Jason R. Rich
www.JasonRich.com

CHAPTER *1*

■ ■ ■

Mortgages:
What You Should Know
to Get Started

WHAT'S IN THIS CHAPTER

- Determine if you are ready to buy a home and take on a mortgage
- The benefits of homeownership
- How does refinancing a mortgage work?
- When refinancing makes sense

■ 1 ■

A s the title suggests, *Mortgages and Refinancing: Get the Best Rates* is all about choosing the best mortgage product to meet your needs and then discovering how to save the most money possible as you shop for the best deals that you qualify for. This book will help you if:

- You're a first-time homebuyer who needs a mortgage
- You're moving from one home to another and require a new mortgage
- You're interested in the potential benefits of refinancing your current mortgage
- You want to cash out, to tap into the equity you have in your home by refinancing, taking on a second mortgage, or applying for a home equity loan

This chapter will help you learn what's involved in obtaining a mortgage. You'll also learn about some of the many lifestyle and financial benefits associated with homeownership. More detailed information about specific types of loans can be found in Chapters 5, 6, and 7.

MORTGAGE TERMS

Refinance (aka refi)—This is the process by which a mortgagor pays off a loan with the proceeds from a new loan, typically using the same property as security for the new loan. The goal is typically to obtain a lower interest rate, reduce the monthly payment, shorten the duration of the loan, or cash out some of the equity.

Equity—This is the current appraised value of your home minus the balance you owe on your mortgage (and/or other loans for

Mortgages and Refinancing: Get the Best Rates

which you used your home as collateral). Thus, if your home is appraised at $200,000 and you owe $150,000 on your mortgage, your equity is $50,000.

Second mortgage—This is a loan a homeowner can obtain in addition to his or her primary mortgage. Just as with a primary mortgage, the home is used as collateral. This second mortgage is totally separate from the first mortgage, with its own rate and terms. The lender for the second mortgage is not entitled to any proceeds from the sale of the home until the lender on the first mortgage has been repaid. Because the risk of default is greater, rates for second mortgages tend to be higher than for first mortgages.

Home equity loan—This is a type of second mortgage that provides the borrower one lump sum of money that he or she must pay back over a specified period of time at a fixed interest rate, using his or her home as collateral. As with a fixed-rate mortgage, the monthly payment on a home equity loan remains constant. Interest rates for home equity loans are typically higher than for mortgages, but lower than for other types of loans, such as credit cards or car loans. The home equity loan has tax benefits, but they're more limited than with a mortgage. Typically, borrowers can deduct interest on home equity loans only up to $100,000. One of the big benefits to this type of loan is that the money can be used for almost anything.

Home equity line of credit (HELOC)—This is a type of second mortgage that provides the borrower with a firm commitment from the lender to make a specified amount of funds available for a specified period of time, using the equity in his or her home as collateral. The difference between a HELOC and a home equity loan is that a HELOC is flexible: during the term of the loan agreement, the borrower can borrow any amount of money up to the credit limit at any time and as often as he or she wants and pay back the outstanding balance over time. HELOCs also differ from home equity loans in that the interest rate is adjustable, not fixed, and the interest is calculated daily. A HELOC has an annual fee. This type of loan can be used as a financial safety net that a homeowner taps only when and if it's needed. This type of loan works more like a credit card than a mortgage.

Are You Ready to Take on the Responsibilities of a Mortgage?

The first step in determining if you could qualify and potentially get approved for a mortgage is to carefully analyze your current financial situation and figure out if this is something you could afford. Using a free calculator on the Ginnie Mae web site (www.ginniemae.gov), you can quickly calculate how much you could potentially afford to spend on your home, assuming you're able to qualify for some type of mortgage.

We'll get into the qualification process shortly. Right now, let's focus on your financial situation to determine if getting approved for a mortgage is within your reach. Many of these same rules apply if you'd like to refinance a mortgage, apply for a second mortgage, or apply for a home equity loan.

Follow these basic steps:

1. *Begin by calculating your total income.* Gather information about all of your current sources of income and calculate your average monthly income. Do you expect this income to remain constant or to increase or decrease in the near future?

2. *Calculate the amount of money you currently have in savings and investments.* This will help you determine how much of a down payment (if any) you can afford. Depending on your situation, you may also need money to cover closing costs and other expenses related to purchasing a home.

3. *Calculate your current monthly expenses.* Are you able to cover all of your living expenses or are you going deeper and deeper into debt? If you're able to cover all of your living expenses and you're able to put some money away into savings, this will greatly improve your chances of qualifying to purchase a home. Keep in mind that once you purchase a home, some of your expenses will go up. For example, you'll need to pay your mortgage (instead of rent), insurance, and property taxes. Some of these added expenses, however, could be offset by the tax benefits associated with homeownership.

4. *Evaluate your current debt.* A potential lender will evaluate your debt in comparison with your income.

5. *Determine your current credit score* and review your credit reports compiled by Experian (www.experian.com), Equifax (www.equifax.com), and TransUnion (www.transunion.com). You should do this two to three months before applying for a mortgage.

MORTGAGE **Credit score**—Using a complex formula that's calculated based
on many criteria related to your current financial situation and
TERMS credit history, the three major credit reporting agencies calculate and regularly update your credit score. Your credit score is based on
such things as your outstanding debt, bill-paying history, and the number and types of accounts you have and how long you have had them.
According to TransUnion, a credit score is "a mathematical calculation
that reflects a consumer's creditworthiness. The score is an assessment
of how likely a consumer is to pay his or her debts."

What to Consider Before Applying for a Mortgage

Some of the financial considerations you'll need to consider
before purchasing a home or acquiring a mortgage include:

- Ensuring that your credit is good enough for you to qualify for a mortgage. Your credit doesn't have to be excellent, but it needs to be at least average—at least 620—for
  you to qualify. (A score in the 700s is ideal for obtaining
  a prime rate loan, which will be discussed later.)

- Being able to show steady employment and a regular
  income. There are ways of obtaining a mortgage without being able to document income. However, you will
  most likely need to provide federal tax returns, W2
  forms, bank statements, and pay stubs to a potential
  lender during the mortgage application process.

- Accruing enough savings to afford a down payment

and cover the costs associated with buying a home. These costs will vary, based on your financial qualifications and the type of mortgage. As a general rule, a down payment of 20 percent or more of the home's purchase price is standard for a conventional loan. However, there are many mortgage options that allow a significantly lower down payment or no down payment at all. There are also ways to obtain a down payment besides tapping your savings. The Federal Housing Administration (FHA) and the Department of Veterans Affairs (VA), for example, have special programs to help qualified first-time home buyers acquire the necessary down payment to purchase a home. If you qualify for an FHA loan (for your mortgage), only a three-percent down payment may be required.

- Ensuring that you'll be able to cover the ongoing costs of home ownership—mortgage payment, insurance, real estate taxes, utility bills, home maintenance and repairs, and so on.

- Making your case to a potential lender, who will carefully analyze your ability to repay the loan, based on income and debt ratio calculations.

The bigger your down payment, the lower your monthly mortgage payments. Your private mortgage insurance (PMI) rates will also be lower and you could qualify for a lower interest rate on the mortgage by

MORTGAGE

HELP

making a larger down payment or prepaying points toward the mortgage. (That's a topic covered later in this book.) Your broker should be able to provide guidance on how to eliminate the need for PMI through the use of second mortgages, home equity lines, or gifts of equity, for example. So, check with your broker before taking on a loan that requires you to pay PMI.

Benefits of Homeownership over Renting

Throughout this book, you will discover many benefits of owning a home as opposed to renting. These benefits include the following:

- As you pay off your mortgage from month to month, you'll be building up equity and increasing your net worth.
- You'll receive significant tax breaks as a homeowner. For example, the interest you pay on your mortgage each year is tax-deductible.
- You'll have control over your home and property and be free to make modifications and improvements without a landlord's approval.
- You'll be able to control your housing costs. With a fixed-rate mortgage, your monthly principal and interest payment will remain constant for the life of the loan. If you're paying rent, however, you can pretty much count on a rent increase from your landlord from time to time.
- You can live out the "American Dream" and own property, which will hopefully go up in value over time.

Principal—This is the amount of money you borrow, not including interest, taxes, or insurance premiums associated with the mortgage.

MORTGAGE

TERMS

Interest rate—This the amount of interest charged on a monthly loan payment, usually expressed as a percentage.

Of course, there's a lot to consider from a financial standpoint before taking on the responsibilities of home ownership. Some of these considerations will be addressed later in this book.

Planning for Your Future

As you're considering whether or not to pursue home ownership, one thing to consider is the real estate market where you want to live. If your job requires you to live in a certain geographic area, make sure that you can qualify for a mortgage and afford a home or condominium in or near that area. Real estate prices may be significantly lower elsewhere in the country, but that doesn't help you if you must live in or near a major city, for example, where real estate prices are exceptionally high.

To evaluate the cost of living and learn about home prices in various places throughout the United States, you can visit these web sites:

- Bankrate.com—www.bankrate.com/brm/movecalc.asp
- CityRating.com—www.cityrating.com/costofliving.asp
- CNN.com—cgi.money.cnn.com/tools/costofliving/costofliving.html

- Sperling's Best Places—www.bestplaces.net/col
- Yahoo! Real Estate—realestate.yahoo.com/re/neighborhood/mail.html

MORTGAGE **HELP**   **Want to live in a more affordable area?** To calculate what your salary could be in another geographic area, based on your current job title and experience, visit the Monster Board web site (promotions.monster.com/salary/) and use the free Salary Wizard.

The term home refers to whichever residence you purchase—whether a single-family house, a multi-family house, an apartment, or a condominium.

If you're planning to relocate or you're not sure what your financial or employment situation will be like in the near future, purchasing a home right now might not be the best strategy for your financial well-being. In addition to using the information in this book, depending on your situation, consider sitting down with a personal financial planner or accountant to help you determine if buying a home in the near future is possible and whether making this type of investment would be beneficial to you.

The Steps Leading to Homeownership

You're about to begin one of the biggest and most expensive projects of your life—finding the perfect home. So much goes into finding the perfect home and purchasing it. For every first-time home buyer, the experience is unique. Your financial situation, personal preferences, needs, and the people you hire to help you through this process (such as your lender/mortgage broker, real estate agent, home inspector, and real estate attorney) will all contribute to your unique home-buying experience.

The following are some of the major steps in buying a home. The order in which you complete these steps, like the real estate professionals you use, will vary. It's important, however, to invest the time necessary to gather all of the right information, analyze your wants and needs carefully, and then ensure that all of your legal and financial interests are protected throughout the entire process. The chapters of this book will help guide you through the steps in the home-buying process:

- Decide where you want to live. Choose a general area, based on your needs, desires, and research into cities, towns, or communities. Start with a wide geographic area and then narrow down your search based on affordability and how much you like a specific community or area, for example.

- Find a reputable and experienced real estate agent. This person will educate you about the area, show you property listings, help you analyze your needs, review your financial situation, and help you negotiate with the seller.

- Determine your wants and needs in a home. How many bedrooms and bathrooms do you need, for example? Are you looking for a single-family home, a multi-family home, a condominium, or an apartment?

- Review your personal financial information to determine exactly what monthly mortgage payment and down payment you can afford.

- Find a lender, bank, credit union, financial institution, or mortgage broker. Then review your financing options with the representative and get prequalified or preapproved for a mortgage. During this process, learn about the many types of mortgage products and financing options available to you, based on your income and credit score.

- Work with a real estate agent, attend open houses, review the real estate section of newspapers, perform searches online, and talk with friends, neighbors, and coworkers to start looking at homes on the market that could meet your needs.

- Formally apply for a mortgage and line up the financing for your home. You'll want to lock in your mortgage rate and terms and then obtain a formal commitment letter from your lender.

- Prepare and submit a written offer to the seller. Your real estate agent or real estate attorney can help you prepare the formal offer.

- Negotiate with the seller to establish the final price and terms of the sale.

- Hire a home inspector to evaluate the home and its current condition. You may also need to hire an appraiser to evaluate the property's current value, based in part on current market conditions.

- Have a purchase and sale agreement (P&S) drawn up and sign it with the seller. Your real estate agent or real estate attorney will help you create an appropriate P&S to meet your needs.
- Start planning your move by packing up your stuff, contacting your landlord, hiring a mover, and so on.
- Obtain homeowner's insurance and the other types of insurance that are required of homeowners. Some types of insurance are optional. Find a reliable insurance agent or broker to help you determine your needs and provide you with appropriate coverage.
- Prepare for the closing—the final step in the home-buying process. This is when all of the documents for the financing and sale get signed and ownership of the home passes from the seller to you. Chapter 8 focuses on the closing process.
- Move into your new home! Get acclimated with your new neighborhood and start your new life as a home-owner.

Each of these major steps in the home-buying process requires the completion of many smaller steps. Some of these will be handled by your real estate agent or other professionals you hire. It will, however, always be your responsibility to provide the people who help and/or represent you with the most timely and accurate information about your finances, personal situation, needs, and desires.

Now that you've obtained a general overview of the steps in the home-buying process, it's time to get started. Keep in mind that this process shouldn't be quick. Each step in this process takes time. For example, plan on spending at least 30 to 60 days searching for your dream home and finding a property that meets your needs and that you can afford. Investing the necessary time, doing research, and asking appropriate questions will help to ensure that you make educated decisions and then wind up happy and comfortable in your new home.

The next chapter focuses on determining if you're qualified for a mortgage and will help you evaluate your personal financial situation, credit history, and credit score. As you'll discover, your credit history and current credit score play a tremendous role in the type of mortgage product you qualify for. This, in turn, relates directly to the fees and interest rate you'll pay to obtain your home financing (mortgage).

The Scoop on Refinancing

If you already have a mortgage, refinancing that mortgage could make a lot of financial sense, depending on your circumstances. The process of refinancing involves three steps. First, you find a new mortgage product with better terms and/or rates than your current mortgage. Then, you apply for that new mortgage and replace your current mortgage with the new mortgage. Finally, with the money you obtain from the new mortgage, your lender immediately pays off your earlier mortgage (after the mandatory three-day rescission period on a refi for a primary residence). Depending on your circumstances, you could also borrow more than you owe on the earlier mortgage in order to obtain cash, based on the equity in your home.

> **Rescission period**—A borrower is allowed to cancel a refinance mortgage within three full days after receiving all required disclosures and signing loan documents. Federal law allows this cancellation (rescission) period for certain loan transactions secured by the borrower's home, but not for loans made to purchase, construct, or acquire a primary residence or to transactions secured by a secondary residence or rental property.

MORTGAGE TERMS

The process of refinancing begins by finding a lender or mortgage broker and then choosing a mortgage product for which your current situation qualifies you. Shopping around for the best rates and deals, choosing a reputable lender or mortgage broker, and then selecting the best mortgage product are equally important steps in the refinancing process.

As you'll discover in Chapter 6, there are a multitude of reasons why someone might choose to refinance. Here are some of these reasons:

- To reduce your interest rate. If interest rates have gone down since you obtained your mortgage, even a slight reduction in your rate through refinancing could reduce your monthly payment and save you a fortune over the life of the loan. Even if interest rates haven't gone down, if your credit score has improved since you obtained your mortgage, you could qualify for better rates and terms.

- To reduce the term of your mortgage. Without increasing your monthly payment, you could go from a 30-year mortgage down to a 15- or 20-year mortgage. This would allow you to pay off your mortgage much sooner and save a fortune in interest over the life of the loan.

- To get cash. If you have a lot of credit card debt, need to make costly improvements to your home, need money for school tuition, or would like additional cash for almost any purpose, by refinancing your home you can potentially also obtain cash, based on your equity. For example, if your home is worth $200,000 (appraised value) and you owe only $150,000 on your current mortgage, this means you have $50,000 of equity against which you could borrow.

MORTGAGE TERMS

Debt consolidation loan—This type of mortgage product allows you to obtain extra cash when you refinance your mortgage and pay off outstanding debt, such as high-interest credit cards or loans. By consolidating debts and loans into one loan with a lower interest rate, you could improve your credit score, save money on interest, and pay off the debt faster. A debt consolidation loan can be part of your new mortgage or you could obtain a separate loan using the equity in your home as collateral.

Cash-out—This is the process of refinancing and borrowing more money than you owe on your current mortgage in order to obtain cash. For example, if you owe $150,000 on your mortgage, but your home's appraised value is $250,000, you could potentially refinance your home and cash out up to $100,000, based on the equity in your home. To refinance, you must meet the lender's requirements for the new mortgage product you apply for. This could mean meeting income/employment requirements, having a specific credit score, and/or having a specified debt ratio or loan-to-value (LTV) ratio.

Other Ways to Tap into the Equity in Your Home

There are several ways to build up equity in your home. You can pay off your mortgage over time, make additional payments toward the principal, or benefit from appreciation of the value of your home. For example, if you purchased your home for $150,000 five years ago and have been paying your mortgage every month, you established equity in your home right away if you made any down payment and, since then, with each monthly mortgage payment (unless you have an interest-only mortgage). At the same time, if the appraised value of your home has increased during those five years, that appreciation in value is also considered equity in your home.

So, you can refinance your mortgage in a way that allows you to cash out, to take equity out of the home in the form of cash by refinancing more than what you owe on your earlier mortgage. You can also use the equity in your home to gain-some cash by obtain a second mortgage, a home equity loan, or a home equity line of credit (HELOC). Depending on your situation, each has its benefits, fees, and potential drawbacks. Which type of loan you use should be based on your needs, current financial situation, credit score, employment situation (income), and ability to shop around for the best loan/mortgage deal. A mortgage broker or lender will be able to help you apply for a second mortgage, home equity loan, or HELOC. You'll learn more about these options in Chapter 7.

Do You Currently Qualify for a Mortgage?

No matter what type of mortgage you apply for, the lender will have a specific list of requirements that you must meet in order to qualify. This also applies to refinancing. The next chapter focuses on how to determine if you'll qualify for a mortgage based on your income, employment situation, credit history, credit score, and down payment (if any).

With so many types of prime and sub-prime mortgage products available, it should be relatively easy for you, with proper research and a knowledgeable mortgage broker or lender, to find a mortgage product you qualify for. If, however, you don't currently qualify, based on what you read in the next chapter, you can figure out what steps you need to take in order to improve your situation so that you can potentially qualify for a mortgage in the not-so-distant future.

☆ ☆ **WARNING** ☆ ☆

Two of the worst mistakes someone can make as a home-owner are allowing his or her credit score to drop significantly and being late on the monthly mortgage payments. Either or both of these mistakes could keep you from refinancing your home or qualifying for a debt consolidation loan or HELOC that could help ease or fix a negative financial situation you experience in the future.

CHAPTER 2

Are You Qualified?

WHAT'S IN THIS CHAPTER

- Analyzing your current financial situation
- Calculating your current debt
- Understanding your credit score and credit history

Mortgages and Refinancing: Get the Best Rates

Back when the only home financing options were fixed-rate mortgages from banks, the qualification and approval requirements were very strict. If you didn't have excellent credit, a well-paying job, money for a down payment, relatively little debt, and a relationship with the local bank, your chances of getting approved were slim or none.

These days, the approval requirements for a mortgage are much easier to meet for many people. This is because there are now so many mortgage options, many types of lenders (decide for banks), and significantly more competition in the mortgage/lending business. While more people than ever before could potentially qualify for a mortgage, the trick is to find a mortgage product that you can afford and that's a good deal for you. Remember: the more risk you bring to the table (due to poor credit, unstable income, lack of down payment, etc.), the higher your interest rate will be and the less desirable the terms of the mortgage. Thus, if your financial situation is currently problematic, taking on a mortgage might not be the most practical move for you right now.

This chapter will help you examine your financial situation and determine if you could potentially qualify for a mortgage. After reading this chapter and completing the financial worksheets provided, consider meeting with several mortgage brokers or lenders to discuss your situation, needs, and goals. Determine which mortgage products, if any, you'd qualify for. Then, crunch the numbers to see if you can afford to take on the monthly financial obligation of a mortgage, along with the taxes, insurance, maintenance, homeowners' association dues (if applicable), and other costs associated with being a homeowner.

Evaluating Your Current Financial Situation

As soon as you begin the mortgage application process, the broker or lender you work with will focus on several aspects of your financial life:

- Your current employment situation and income
- Your current debt and financial obligations
- Your current savings, investments, and assets
- Your credit history and credit score

MORTGAGE **There are mortgage products** suitable for people with bad credit, unstable income, and/or little or no savings that can

HELP be applied to a down payment. So, if one or two of these areas is weak, you could still potentially qualify for a mortgage.

If you have a co-borrower, such as a spouse, the lender will evaluate all of his or her financial information as well.

The following worksheet will help you better understand your finances. It's important to review your current situation and understand where you stand. Embellishing any numbers, failing to mention negative information, or not fully focusing on your entire financial picture will only result in additional work and stress when applying for a mortgage, plus increase the chances that your application will be rejected. You're much better off being totally truthful about your situation and then pursuing a mortgage product you actually qualify for.

Gather up your current bank statements, pay stubs, tax returns (if self-employed), bills, credit card statements, and other financial paperwork. Then complete the following financial worksheet to the best of your ability.

Financial Worksheet

Income	Dollars
Current Salary (including any tips, commissions, and bonuses)	$
Co-Borrower s Salary	$
Other Sources of Income (such as interest, alimony, child support, and investment dividends)	$
Total Average Monthly Income:	$

Your monthly income is used to help determine what type of mortgage product you'd qualify for and how much the lender will be willing to make available to you, based on your ability to make the monthly payments. Use the chart on the next page to calculate these expenses.

A lender will be looking at the principal, interest, taxes, insurance, and homeowners' association dues (if applicable) on the property you intend to purchase or refinance. The lender will use this information to determine your monthly

Monthly Expenses	Dollars
Car Expenses (monthly car payments, gas, repairs, insurance, etc.)	$
Child Support	$
Clothing	$
Entertainment	$
Food	$
Gifts	$
Insurance (health insurance, car insurance, life insurance, renter's insurance, etc.)	$
Medical Expenses	$
Rent	$
Utilities (electricity, gas, phone, cable, etc.)	$
Travel/Vacations	$
Other Expenses	$
Total Monthly Expenses:	**$**

housing expenses. To determine your total debts, the lender will use these items, plus the monthly minimum payments due on all of your installment/revolving debt (car loans, car leases, credit cards, student loans, etc.). The information about your debts will normally be taken directly from your credit report and you will not need to document these debts for the lender.

The worksheet provided in this book is to help you get a good understanding of your total living expenses, so you can budget your new mortgage expenses accordingly.

After obtaining information about a potential loan from a broker or lender, crunch the numbers and make sure the monthly payment for that loan can fit in your current monthly budget. Remember: you need to be able to afford your monthly mortgage payment, but you also need to eat as well.

☆ ☆ **WARNING** ☆ ☆

When deciding how large of a loan you qualify for, a lender will *not* take into consideration all of the expenses listed on this worksheet, but it is important for you to budget for these expenses as well.

**Current *Monthly* Payment Due on
All Debt and Debt-Related Expenses**

Monthly Expenses	Dollars
Alimony	$
Car Loan(s)	$
Child Support	$
Credit Cards (Minimum Payments)	$
Outstanding Medical Bills	$
School/Education Loans	$
Other Debt	$
Total Monthly Debt and Debt-Related Expenses:	$

Lenders and brokers will also calculate and potentially evaluate your monthly debt and current expense obligations, relative to your income, in order to make their approval decision for a mortgage.

Savings	Dollars
Checking Account Balance(s)	$
Investments (stocks, mutual funds, etc.)	$
Retirement Fund Contribution(s)	$
Savings Account Balance(s)	$
Other Savings	$
Total Savings:	**$**

The amount of your savings, investments, and other assets will help a lender or mortgage broker determine how much of a down payment you could make when purchasing a home. The amount you have available for a down payment (compared with the purchase price) will help determine what mortgage products, interest rate, and loan terms you qualify for. Your savings and investments will also be used to help determine if you can afford your monthly financial obligations.

MORTGAGE HELP **Once you take on the responsibilities** associated with a mortgage, some of the additional expenses you'll be incurring are your monthly mortgage payment (which replaces your rent payment), homeowner's insurance (which replaces your renter's insurance), property taxes, utility costs, mortgage insurance, and condominium/homeowners' association fees (if any).

As you begin searching for your dream home and applying for financing, one of the things lenders will consider is your ability to afford and make timely mortgage payments. Two figures that will be considered are your *PITI* and *PITIO*. The *PITI* represents the *principal*, *interest*, *property taxes*, and *insurance* costs associated with your mortgage's monthly payment. The *PITIO* represents the principal, interest, property taxes, insurance, and your other monthly expenses.

In terms of these ratio calculations, there are two that lenders will be focusing on—your *front ratio* and your *back ratio*.

Your *front ratio* is your monthly principal, interest, taxes, and insurance divided by your gross monthly income. (If you have a co-borrower, the information about both parties is calculated for this ratio.) This is also called your *housing expense ratio.*

Monthly PITI Front Ratio = _____
Gross Monthly Income

Your *back ratio* is the sum of your monthly PITI and your monthly minimum debt payments divided by your gross monthly income. Also called your *debt ratio,* it is used to determine your *debt-to-income ratio* (DTI).

Monthly PITI + Monthly Minimum Debt Payments
Back Ratio = _____
Gross Monthly Income

For both front and back ratios, the lower the number, the less risky the loan is for the lender and the better your chances of qualifying for the loan. A good mortgage broker may be able to teach you strategies for improving your ratios.

Review Your Credit Reports and Obtain Your Credit Score

Now that you've reviewed your current financial situation, let's take a look at your *credit history* and *credit score*. These are two extremely important pieces of information virtually every lender will carefully examine. By doing some work on your own, you can take steps right away to improve your credit score, which will make you a more appealing borrower to many lenders/brokers.

MORGAGE *Credit score*—This is a number representing a person's creditworthiness, calculated by the three major credit reporting agencies, using a complex formula based on many criteria related to the person's current financial situation and credit history, and updated regularly. Your credit score or your credit rating is based on such things as your outstanding debt, bill-paying history, and the number and types of accounts you have and how long you have had them. According to TransUnion, a credit score is "a mathematical calculation that reflects a consumer's creditworthiness. The score is an assessment of how likely a consumer is to pay his or her debts."

TERMS

Credit report—Compiled by one of the credit reporting agencies—Equifax, Experian, or TransUnion—a credit report contains personal and financial information about you, including your name, address, phone number, Social Security number, date of birth, past addresses, current and past employers, companies that have issued you credit (including credit cards, charge cards, car loans, mortgages, student loans, home equity loans, etc.), and details about your credit history (whether or not you pay your bills on time). Each of the major credit reporting agencies compiles a separate credit report for every individual. However, much of the information on each report should be identical or extremely similar.

Credit reporting agency (aka credit bureau)—One of the three national bureaus that maintain credit reports on virtually all Americans with any type of credit history—Equifax, Experian, and TransUnion. These agencies maintain vast databases that are updated regularly. Their purpose is to supply creditors with timely and reliable financial information about individual consumers. It's important to understand that a credit reporting agency does *not* decide whether an individual qualifies for credit or not. Credit reporting agencies simply collect information that is relevant to a person's credit history and habits and then provides that information (for a fee), in the form of a credit report, to creditors and lenders.

Start reviewing your credit history by contacting the credit reporting agencies (credit bureaus) and obtain a current copy of your credit report from each agency—Experian (www. experian.com), Equifax (www.equifax.com), and TransUnion (www.transunion.com).

The easiest way to do this (for free) is to visit the AnnualCreditReport.com web site (www.annualcreditreport. com). This is a web site sponsored by the three credit reporting agencies and approved by the U.S. government. Beware of imposter web sites with similar URLs that claim to offer a free copy of your credit report, but charge you to become a member of the company's credit monitoring service, for example.

The AnnualCreditReport.com web site provides your credit reports for free, but charges a small fee for your credit score. Tips for how to obtain your credit score follow later in this chapter.

MORTGAGE HELP **Another way to obtain** all three of your credit reports, along with corresponding credit scores, without doing any work yourself, is to contact a mortgage broker and start the mortgage prequalification process. The broker will then obtain your credit reports and credit scores and will typically provide you with copies of this information for free, if you ask.

MORTGAGE TERMS *AnnualCreditReport.com*—This is a centralized service operated by the three credit reporting agencies (credit bureaus) that processes all requests from consumers who wish to receive their free credit report from each agency. This can be done online, by phone, or by mail. To obtain your annual credit report, visit www.annualcreditreport.com.

While it costs nothing to obtain a copy of your credit report from each credit bureau once every 12 months, you will need to pay to obtain your official *credit score*, the number that all brokers and lenders use as an indicator of your creditworthiness, to help determine what type of mortgage product you'd qualify for. Each credit bureau will assign you a score based on information that appears in your credit report as compiled by that credit bureau.

Mortgages and Refinancing: Get the Best Rates

A credit score is a three-digit number between 300 and 850. A credit score in the 300s or 400s indicates a history of being an extremely high credit risk, a score in the mid-600s to low 700s indicates a good credit risk, and a credit score in the mid- to high 700s or in the 800s is considered an excellent credit risk. People with these higher credit scores tend to get the best deals in terms of low interest rates, for example, when applying for a mortgage, loan, or credit card.

To qualify for a mortgage at a decent rate and with favorable terms, you'll want your credit score to be at least 620, although there are mortgage products available for people with scores in the 500s. The average credit score in America is 678.

It's important to remember that different lenders and creditors give different weight to these scores. When making a decision to approve a loan or credit, here's how credit scores are generally perceived by lenders and creditors:

Excellent	Over 750
Very Good	720 to 750
Acceptable (Average)	660 to 719
Uncertain	620 to 659
High risk	Less than 619

Knowing your credit score before you apply for a mortgage will help you determine whether or not you'll easily qualify for a mortgage or if you'll have to shop around to find sub-prime lenders willing to approve mortgages for people with average or below-average credit, at higher interest rates.

Obtain Your Credit Score from Each Credit Bureau

Each of the three credit bureaus will assign you a credit score based on the information that appears on your credit report compiled by that bureau. As information on your credit report changes, so does your credit score.

You can use the AnnualCreditReport.com web site to obtain your credit reports or you can visit the web site of each credit bureau. You can also call each credit bureau or send your request via mail, but this takes significantly longer. To obtain your credit report, you will need to provide your full name, address, phone number, date of birth, and Social Security number.

What's Your Credit Score?

Current Credit Score from Equifax: _____

Current Credit Score from Experian: _____

Current Credit Score from TransUnion: _____

The information on your credit report includes details about your current credit status, your payment history, and other pertinent data a creditor or lender can use to make intelligent decisions about whether or not to grant you credit or a loan, such as a mortgage. In the past, for a creditor to make this decision required a person with specialized training to carefully analyze all of the information on your credit report manually and then make a determination. That was how things were done about two decades ago. Today, thanks to computers, the process is far more automated and mortgage prequalification decisions can be made in minutes, not hours or days, thanks to the introduction of credit scoring.

Using only information that's found on your credit report, a complex mathematical algorithm is used to calculate a credit score based on a variety of criteria, each of which is weighted differently. The resulting number represents how much of a credit risk you are as a consumer.

While you're entitled to a free copy of your credit report every 12 months, the credit reporting agencies are not obligated to provide you with your credit score for free. Instead, they charge you for it. When you request a free copy of your credit report, you may receive an offer to purchase your corresponding credit score and receive the report and score at the same time. For this, you'll be charged approximately $6 per score.

You can also contact each of the three credit reporting agencies separately to purchase your credit score in conjunction with a credit report or separately. For example, from Experian, you can purchase a single credit report and corresponding credit score for $15 or just your credit score for $5.95.

Your credit score is sometimes called your *FICO® Score*. FICO® is a registered trademark of Fair Isaac Corporation (NYSE:FIC), the pioneer of the FICO® credit score that's used by many lenders to evaluate consumer credit risk. According to the company's web site, "Credit reporting agency risk scores produced from models developed by Fair Isaac Corporation are commonly known as FICO® Scores. Fair Isaac credit reporting agency scores are used by lenders and others to assess the credit risk of prospective borrowers or existing customers, in order to help make credit and marketing decisions. These scores are derived solely from the information available on credit reporting agency reports. For a fee, you can obtain your FICO® Score online at www.MyFICO.com.

MORTGAGE **It's definitely a good idea** to purchase your credit score when you obtain a copy of your credit report. Simply by **HELP** reviewing your credit report, it's virtually impossible for you to calculate or even estimate your corresponding credit score, yet this is a vital piece of information that will ultimately determine whether or not you're credit worthy.

Each of the credit reporting agencies (Experian, Equifax, and TransUnion) maintains a credit report on every consumer. The information on each credit report is often slightly different, because not all creditors and lenders report data to all three credit bureaus. Thus, when you review your three credit reports side by side, you'll often notice small discrepancies. This is totally normal. Because your credit score is calculated by the data on each credit report, each of your credits scores will also be slightly different.

If your three credit scores are different, a lender will use the middle score to initially determine your eligibility for a mortgage and your interest rate. If you only have two scores available, the lower score will be used. (If you are applying with a spouse or co-borrower, the lender will use the lower of either one of your middle scores.)

When obtaining your credit score, make sure the number you buy and receive is your official FICO® Credit Score. More than 70 percent of all lenders use an official FICO® Credit Score to make their lending and credit approval decisions.

When you apply for a major credit card or a store credit card, for example, that creditor will check your credit history by reviewing your credit report from one of the credit-reporting agencies. Which agency they use (Experian, Equifax, or TransUnion) is their decision. In many cases, when you get a credit decision in under five minutes, that decision is based exclusively on your credit score that went along with the credit report accessed. The quick approval or rejection was an entirely automated process.

When you apply for a more substantial loan, such as a mortgage, the mortgage broker or finance company (lender) will typically access all three of your credit reports, then use the middle credit score to help make an approval decision.

Because the information on your credit report constantly changes, as creditors report new or updated data and old data (over seven years old) drops off your credit report, your credit score from each credit-reporting agencies also changes. If you're late making credit card or loan payments, for example, your credit score could drop significantly. After your score takes a dip, it's much harder and often takes longer for it to rise again.

It's an excellent strategy to review your credit reports 60 to 90 days before applying for a mortgage. This gives you ample time to have any errors

MORTGAGE
HELP

on your report corrected and to take steps to clean up your credit report before it's reviewed by potential lenders. Any incorrect or out-of-date information listed on your credit report could be dragging your credit score down. When applying for a mortgage, you want your credit score to be as high as possible so you qualify for the best deals and interest rates.

In addition to fixing information that's incorrectly stated on your credit report(s), here are other ways to improve your credit score:

- Pay all of your bills, including credit cards, car loans, etc., on time for at least 12 months. If you currently have a mortgage, it is vital to that you never make any payments late.

- Keep your credit card balances low. Ideally, your balance on each credit card should be no higher than 35 percent of your credit limit. Also, make timely monthly payments on the balance that are above the required monthly minimums.

- Do not close old or unused accounts that appear on your credit reports, but that are in good standing.

- For several months prior to applying for a mortgage, do not apply for any new credit cards or car loans or do anything else to increase your debt dramatically.

- Avoid excessive inquiries to the credit bureaus. Within a 30- to 45-day period, any number of lenders or mortgage brokers can obtain your credit report with no penalty against your credit score. However, every time a different type of lender, such as a credit card company, department store, or car dealership, pulls your credit report, your credit score will drop slightly for as long as several months.

- Don't consolidate credit card balances onto one card and come close to reaching your credit limit on that one card. In terms of your credit score, you're better off maintaining lower balances on several cards and keeping all of your accounts up-to-date by paying at least your monthly minimums.

- If negative but accurate information appears on your credit report, contact each of your creditors directly and negotiate to have the negative information removed. This will often require paying off your debt or at least bringing your account up-to-date. The lender or creditor that placed negative information on your credit report can remove it. Getting the company to agree to do this isn't always easy, however.

For additional advice on boosting your credit score, be sure to read *Dirty Little Secrets: How to Clean Up Your Credit Report and Boost Your FICO Score* (Jason R. Rich, Entrepreneur Press, 2006). This book is an excellent resource for learning how to obtain, review, and—if necessary—fix your credit report and improve your credit score before you apply for a mortgage.

MORTGAGE

HELP

After reviewing your financial situation, completing the

Financial Worksheet earlier in this chapter, reviewing your credit reports, and obtaining your credit score, set up meetings with several mortgage brokers, banks, lenders, credit unions, and/or other financial institutions to discuss your home financing options. You'll definitely want to shop around and initially talk with several mortgage specialists—first to determine your options and then to find the very best deals available based on your credit score and current financial situation.

The Next Step: Meeting with Mortgage Brokers and Lenders

Now that you have a good idea of your current financial situation, meeting with several mortgage brokers or lenders is the next step toward getting a mortgage or refinancing your current mortgage. In the next chapter, you'll discover strategies for finding the most qualified, knowledgeable, experienced, and trustworthy broker or lender and discover what financial paperwork you'll need to provide in the mortgage application process.

In addition to choosing the best type of mortgage to meet your needs, finding the right lender or mortgage broker to work with could save you a tremendous amount of frustration, time, and money.

CHAPTER 3

Choosing a Mortgage Broker or Lender

WHAT'S IN THIS CHAPTER

- Learn how to identify the best broker or lender
- Information needed to choose a broker or lender
- Putting a home-buying team together

A mortgage broker is a home financing expert. He or she represents a variety of lenders and can help you choose the best mortgage product to meet your needs, plus help you with the entire mortgage application and approval process. While most home buyers and people looking to refinance their mortgage work with a mortgage broker, your other option is to work directly with a lender (such as a bank, credit union, savings and loan, mortgage company, or some other financial institution) to help you obtain the mortgage or home financing you desire.

TIP: Over 80 percent of the home buyers in the U.S. work through a mortgage broker. As of 2005, there were over 20,000 mortgage brokerage companies in America.

This chapter will help you find the best mortgage broker or lender to work with, based on your needs. You'll also learn how to avoid common pitfalls people often encounter when shopping for a loan.

While a mortgage is a product that you'll be shopping for (and looking to get the best terms and rates for), the process of finding the right mortgage broker or lender to work with involves hiring someone who will be performing a valuable service for you. As you'll discover, in addition to helping you choose the most suitable mortgage product to apply for, a mortgage broker will also perform a wide range of other services on your behalf.

Finding the Right Broker or Lender

In three words, the trick to obtaining the best mortgage is to *shop, compare* and *negotiate* with the lender or broker you ultimate decide to work with. That lender could be a local bank, credit union, a mortgage company or some other type of financial institution. As you'll discover, various organizations (such as mortgage brokers) specialize in different types of mortgage products that are suitable for different types of borrowers. Virtually all lenders are happy to work with people with excellent credit and a steady, well-paying job. If, however, you don't fall into this category (and plenty of people don't), you may need to spend some extra time shopping around for the best lender or mortgage broker to work with, in order to obtain an approval and receive the best possible rates and overall deal.

> **MORTGAGE TERMS**
>
> *Loan officer (*aka *broker associate* or *mortgage consultant)*—The person who works for the mortgage broker who is your primary contact person through application, approval, and closing can have any of several job titles. Their job description, however, is basically the same—to work with you, the borrower, and help you choose a mortgage product, help you apply for the mortgage and get approved by the lender, and prepare you for the closing. The loan officer will often work on a commission, based on the mortgage product he or she sells.

☆ ☆ **WARNING** ☆ ☆

The mortgage broker you work with should never encourage you to provide false information or inaccurate financial documents to the lender, nor should you be encouraged to leave signature lines blank on any application or loan forms. The mortgage broker should be open and honest when explaining all of the fees associated with the loan, including what they charge for their services.

Banks, credit unions, savings and loans, and many other types of financial institutions offer only their own mortgage products. As a result, their offerings and ability to negotiate rates may be limited due to these limitations and strict guidelines. Because a mortgage broker represents multiple lenders, there's a lot more flexibility in terms of what they offer and charge. A typical mortgage broker will handle these tasks:

- Assess the borrower's circumstances and evaluate his or her credit history and employment situation (income) as appropriate.
- Help the borrower find the best mortgage product to fit their needs, based on current rates and offerings by various lenders. This includes educating the borrower about the various financing options available to them.
- Assist the borrower in getting pre-approved for a mortgage with one of their lenders.

- Gather all documentation (bank statements, pay stubs, W-2 forms, etc.) on behalf of the lender.
- Work with the borrower to complete the application form(s) for the mortgage.
- Submit the application and appropriate financial documents to the lender
- Work as the liaison between the borrower and lender throughout the application processing and closing process.

When you start shopping around for a mortgage, you'll quickly discover that different lenders and mortgage brokers will quote you different prices and rates for what appears to be the same type of loan. When comparing offers from lenders or brokers, make sure you know the loan amount, loan term, and the type of loan, so you can easily compare the quoted fees and rates. Other things you'll need to determine when evaluating an offer from a lender or broker is whether or not the rate is fixed or adjustable. If you're taking on an adjustable-rate mortgage and interest rates go up, so will your monthly payment. Meanwhile, depending on the terms of your loan, your monthly payment might not drop, even if interest rates fall.

Be sure to determine the loan's *annual percentage rate (APR)*. The APR takes into account the interest rate and points, brokers fees, and other fees associated with the loan. *Points* are fees you may pay to the lender or broker; a point is one percent of the loan amount. Typically, the more points you pay, the lower your interest rate on the mortgage will be.

When a lender or broker is describing a mortgage product, ask for the points to be expressed in dollars, so you can easily determine what you're responsible to pay.

MORTGAGE **TERMS** *Annual percentage rate (APR)*—This is the yearly rate of interest that includes all fees and costs paid to acquire the loan (such as interest, mortgage insurance, certain closing costs, and points paid at closing). All lenders are obligated by law to disclose a loan's APR. When comparing fixed-rate mortgages, compare the APRs, not just the interest rates or the monthly payments.

Point—This is a fee the borrower pays to the lender or broker. It's one percent of the loan amount.

Fees are another component of a mortgage you need to be concerned about. As you'll discover, when you take on a mortgage, a wide range of fees are involved. When you begin working with a broker or lender, be sure to ask for a summary of all fees you'll be responsible for paying. Otherwise, at the closing, you could be surprised at how much you're paying and realize you could have negotiated those fees down if you had learned about them sooner. Some of the fees you'll have to pay when you apply for the mortgage. Other fees will be due at closing or built into the loan.

Another question to ask the lender or broker early on is about the size of the down payment required to get the mortgage application approved. Depending on the type of mortgage, the down payment required could be anywhere from zero to 20 percent of the purchase price. Of course, the more money you offer as a down payment, the lower the amount of your mortgage and, thus, the lower your monthly payment.

Interest rates for mortgages change daily. The deal you discuss on a Monday, for example, most likely will not still be available on the following Thursday or Friday, unless you take steps to lock in the rate with the lender or broker. Likewise, the same loan could be offered at different rates to different people, based on their credit histories and credit scores.

It's important to review the fees charged by the lender or broker early on and negotiate to have as many of them waived or reduced as possible in order to save money. Not all fees can be waived or reduced, but many of them can. It's these fees that often determine the profit for the lender or broker. Once you negotiate all of the fees, make sure that no fees are added and that your interest rate and/or the points you're required to pay don't increase. After you've reached an agreement with the lender or broker, you should obtain a written lock-in to ensure what you've agreed to will be binding.

The lock-in should specify the rate, summarize the fees, and state the period the lock-in will last. At this point, you may be charged a fee to lock in your rate. If rates rise before your closing, you will be protected. However, unless you negotiate this in advance, if rates fall, you could wind up paying a higher rate. Before locking in a rate, inquire about your broker/lender's *float down policy*. What this means is that, as a courtesy to you, good lenders will automatically reduce your locked-in rate, without a fee, if rates go down by a quarter percent or more within your lock-in period.

If your credit is average or below average, you may be forced to work with a higher-cost lender who will charge you extra fees and offer you a higher interest rate, because you represent a greater risk based upon your credit history. If you have unusual circumstances relating to your personal finances and credit history, it's important that your lender or mortgage broker understand your situation before recommending specific mortgage products to you.

One way to potentially improve your chances of getting the best rates is to review your credit report early on and take steps to correct any inaccuracies or outdated information that could be negatively impacting your credit score. If your credit report has negative information that is hurting your credit score, consider paying off your creditors and/or negotiating with them to have the negative information modified or removed.

In the next chapter, you will learn about some of the many types of mortgage products available, such as fixed-rate loans, adjustable-rate loans, nontraditional loans, interest-only loans, and jumbo loans. If you understand the differences among these products, you can choose which one best meets your individual needs. Once you determine this, you can shop around several lenders or brokers to find the best possible rates.

☆ ☆ **WARNING** ☆ ☆

According to Wikipedia (en.wikipedia.org/wiki/Mortgage_broker), "Another unethical practice involves inserting hidden clauses in contracts in which a borrower will unknowingly promise to pay the broker or lender to find him or her a mortgage whether or not the mortgage is closed. Though regarded as unethical by the National Association of Mortgage Brokers, this practice is perfectly legal. Often a dishonest lender will convince the consumer that he or she is signing an application and nothing else. Often the consumer will not hear again from the lender until after the time expires and then they are forced to pay all costs. Potential borrowers may even be sued without having legal defense."

Choosing Your Lender or Broker

Finding a mortgage broker or lender is easy. They advertise everywhere! The trick, however, is finding someone who is reputable, extremely knowledgeable, and willing to work with you and invest the necessary time to help you get the best deal possible based on your personal situation. It's always a good idea to get a referral from a friend, neighbor, co-worker, or relative. Otherwise, you can find lenders and mortgage brokers online; advertising in newspapers, on radio, or on television; in the Yellow Pages; or through a referral from your real estate agent.

MORTGAGE

HELP

Seriously consider participating in a free workshop offered by the U.S. Department of Housing and Urban Development (HUD). These workshops are offered throughout the United States on an ongoing basis. To learn more, call (800) 569-4287, or visit www.hud.gov/buying/localbuying.cfm.

The Mortgage Bankers Association (www.mortgagebankers.org) is a professional trade association of lenders and mortgage brokers. The organization publishes guidelines and requirements for its members. The "MBA Best Practices" guidelines can be found on the organization's web site. If your mortgage broker is a member of this organization, it's a good idea to review these best practices to ensure that he or she is adhering to them. They relate to compliance with state and federal laws, training, equitable treatment of clients, pricing, advertising and marketing guidelines, and other factors that can impact a borrower.

MORTGAGE

TERMS

Mortgage banker—There are many types of lenders (also referred to as *mortgagees*) who offer mortgages, such as a bank, credit union, or savings and loan. Another type of lender is a mortgage banker. This is a company or individual who uses their own funds to lend money. Many mortgage bankers have their own mortgage approval guidelines and requirements that may be more flexible or lenient than a traditional bank, for example. Mortgage brokers typically represent a handful of mortgage bankers and other types of lenders.

Before committing to work with a lender or broker, check this person out with your local Chamber of Commerce and/or the Better Business Bureau (www.bbb.org). A lender or broker may advertise the best rates or make appealing statements in his or her ads, but those statements might not be true or what's offered might not be best suited to meet your needs. You'll often find that the brokers and lenders that advertise the most and have the catchiest radio and TV jingles also charge the highest fees, and they don't necessarily offer the personalized service you'll want and need, whether you're buying a home or looking to refinance.

There are many free online mortgage comparison shopping sites. When you use one of these services, you'll be required to enter all of your pertinent personal and financial information. Those details will then be forwarded to a handful of potential brokers or lenders who will prequalify you and compete for your business. If you choose to utilize one of these services, you can expect to be bombarded by telemarketing phone calls, e-mails, and direct mail from potential lenders and brokers soliciting your business. While this can make shopping for the best deal easier, it can also get frustrating and annoying, since some brokers and lenders will be relentless in trying to do business with you.

Here are several popular online mortgage comparison shopping sites:

- Bankrate.com—www.bankrate.com
- HomeGain.com—www.homegain.com
- LendingTree.com—www.lendingtree.com
- LowerMyBills.com—www.lowermybills.com

As you choose your lender or broker, these should be your four primary concerns:

1. The broker can get your loan processed on time and has a good working relationship with lenders. You don't want your deal to fall through because the broker misrepresented his or her ability to get the loan approved and closed within a specified time.
2. The lender or broker has competitive rates.
3. The lender or broker is willing to offer you the best possible deal you qualify for, regardless of how much he or she earns in commissions and fees from the transaction.
4. The lender or broker you choose is knowledgeable and trustworthy.

MORTGAGE **Ask your bank, mortgage company,** or broker about your *mortgage par rate.* This is the best mortgage rate you qual-
HELP ify to receive, based on your credit score and credit history (information on your credit reports). Ask if they are getting a *yield spread premium* for increasing your interest rate over par. If the answer is yes, this will help you determine how much the lender and/or broker is earning.

Meet Mortgage Consultant Mark Giordani

Mark Giordani is a senior mortgage consultant with one of the largest privately owned mortgage brokerage firms and correspondent lenders in the United States. Acting as a personal "mortgage shopper," his job is to help his clients determine their mortgage needs and apply for the most suitable mortgage and then to oversee the mortgage process—from pre-qualification to closing.

Because he works for a well-established and large mortgage brokerage and correspondent lender, he has access to dozens of lenders offering hundreds of mortgage products. In this interview, Giordani offers advice to home buyers and homeowners looking to refinance on the mortgage application process and working with a broker. In Chapters 5 and 7, Giordani offers advice about specific types of mortgage and home financing products and whom they'll interest most.

Based in Massachusetts, Giordani works with a broad range of clients from across America. His firm offers an abundance of streamlined documentation loans that eliminate the need for the borrower to provide asset and income documentation. These reduced documentation loans can save the borrower a tremendous amount of time and hassle. Giordani can be reached at (888) 695-3353 or (508) 291-8000.

What is a mortgage broker?

Mark Giordani: "A mortgage broker is just like a Realtor®, except instead of helping you find the perfect home, a mortgage broker helps you find the perfect home financing option, based upon your unique situation. The mortgage broker's job is to collect specific information from you, then unitize that information to find you the best mortgage product you'd qualify for. The benefit of working with a broker is that they have relationships with many different lenders, so they typically have access to a much broader range of mortgage products. If you work with a bank or a mortgage lender directly, you're limited to only the mortgage products offered by that one company."

What's the best way to find a reputable and knowledgeable mortgage broker?

Mark Giordani: "The very best way to find a mortgage broker is through a referral from someone you know and trust, who has had a good working relationship with their broker. Positive word-of-mouth referrals are one of the main ways I acquire new clients. If you can't find a good referral from someone you know, sit down with three or four different brokers before choosing one to work with."

Is there anything that makes one mortgage brokerage different from another?

Mark Giordani: "There are many things that distinguish one mortgage brokerage firm from another. The first is size. Most often, the larger mortgage brokerage firms do more volume of business with the banks they represent. This often means that they have lower rates that can be passed on to you. In addition, larger mortgage brokerage firms tend to be licensed in more states. You have to be sure that the company you are working with meets the appropriate licensing guidelines in your state. Also, many mortgage brokerage firms function as 'correspondent lenders.' What this means is that the mortgage brokerage company is actually going to close your loan in the name of their company. It also means that your entire loan process from application to processing to underwriting and closing will all be done in house.

MORTGAGE TERMS

Correspondent lender—In addition to mortgage brokers and direct lenders, you'll also find hybrid companies that offer borrowers the benefits of working with a direct lender and the flexibility of working with a broker who represents many mortgage products. A correspondent lender makes approval decisions and initially funds the loan, as a mortgage banker or direct lender would. Upon closing the loan, however, the correspondent lender then sells the loan to another lender for servicing. As the borrower, you'll be dealing with the banker who will be funding your loan right from the start, yet who will be able to shop your mortgage around to find you the best rates and terms. Typically, a correspondent lender will offer more competitive rates than ordinary brokers. When shopping around for a broker or lender, ask if the company is a correspondent lender.

"Working with a broker that is also an established 'correspondent lender' can offer you big advantages, not only in rates and terms, but also in speed and efficiency. Because the brokerage company is functioning directly as a lender, they can identify problems much earlier in the process that would otherwise not be caught until later with other firms. Look for a correspondent lender as your broker whenever possible. If timing is critical, correspondents can get things done cheaper and faster than their broker counterparts."

What type of personal or financial information should a borrower be prepared to provide during an initial conversation with a mortgage broker?

Mark Giordani: "During the initial conversation, provide as much basic information about your unique situation as possible. This doesn't mean, however, that you must provide all of the details pertaining to your personal financial information right away. At some point, you will need to provide your date of birth and Social Security number so the broker can review your credit, but this should happen after you develop a comfort level working with that broker. Initially, your broker should be provided with an overview of what you hope to do. In other words, just tell them what your plans are."

Should a first-time home buyer seek out a prequalification before starting the mortgage application process?

Mark Giordani: "I recommend getting prequalified as a first step, because this will make you a more attractive buyer to Realtors® and sellers. Once you go through the prequalification process and then start looking for a home to purchase, you should begin the pre-approval or full mortgage application process. While a mortgage company will do an analysis to determine how much house you can afford, I don't recommend trusting their numbers. In reality, what the banks and lenders do is determine the *maximum* that they are willing to lend to you. The banks do not take into consideration that you may want to be paying for other things than just your mortgage. They do not consider that you may want to be saving for school tuitions or that you want to be able to take vacations or go out to eat. You have to determine how much you want to afford for your new home.

"A good broker can help you, but ultimately, it is your money. You know best what kind of lifestyle you want to have after you purchase your new home. Don't let any lender tell you how much to spend on a new home."

What services should someone expect from his or her mortgage broker?

Mark Giordani: "One of the biggest complaints people have about some mortgage brokers is their lack of accessibility and follow-through. They're too busy to return phone calls and they're never available to answer questions. A good mortgage broker is someone you should be able to pick up the phone and call. If you need to leave a message, it should be returned in a timely fashion. If you find a mortgage broker isn't attentive to your needs, find someone else to work with right away.

"It is helpful to know that a mortgage broker's job is a very active one and a good mortgage broker can go from very available to extremely busy within just few days, based on rapidly changing market conditions and the number of closings they might have in a given week. If you generally find your mortgage broker to be responsive, do not panic if he takes a little extra time to return a particular call. Mortgage brokers juggle the needs of many clients simultaneously and develop a sense of prioritizing to handle truly urgent issues. Sometimes less time-sensitive matters need to wait.

"That being said, find someone who is willing to take the time to answer all of your questions. Many people are under the impression that when they work with a mortgage broker, they're simply buying a product—the mortgage. This isn't the case. They're also buying a service. It's the service the mortgage broker provides that'll help the borrower choose a mortgage product, complete the application-and-approval process, and oversee the entire home-financing process from start to finish. The borrower's goal should be to establish a working relationship with their broker. Find someone who is willing to invest the time needed to answer all of your questions. If someone is reluctant to educate you, address your concerns, and answer your questions, seek out a different broker immediately."

How much discretion does a mortgage company have when it comes to determining your interest rate and fees?

Mark Giordani: "Banks and lenders look for different things in terms of the qualifications of the borrower. Lenders make their approval decisions based on three things: the borrower's credit, collateral, and character. The credit information comes directly from the credit bureaus. The collateral is determined by your down payment and the value of the property being purchased. This is why an appraisal is usually needed. The borrower's character refers to such factors as your past housing history and employment history. These three factors combined will help determine the interest rate and loan terms a lender is willing to offer the borrower.

"If someone's credit is challenged due to late payments on a car loan, student loan, or credit cards, for example, this may negatively impact the rate the borrower is going to be offered. The loan-to-value calculation will also help determine the interest rate. If the borrower is making a large down payment, this will often allow the lender to offer a better interest rate or more desirable terms. Essentially, as the risk goes up for the lender, the higher the interest you're going to pay.

> *Loan-to-value (LTV)*—This is the ratio between the amount of the loan and the value of the property. Many types of mortgages have a specific LTV as a requirement for approval. If you're buying a home and making a 20-percent down payment, your LTV would be 80 percent. If you're making a five-percent down payment, your LTV would be 95 percent.

MORTGAGE

TERMS

"Within a specific person's scenario, the broker does have some discretion on the rate and terms offered. This is, in part, based on how much profit the broker wants to earn. It's important for the borrower to understand that, while the rate and some fees are often somewhat negotiable, not all fees are negotiable. There are definite limits as to how much discretion a broker has. Many of the fees that are charged on a loan transaction are actual out-of-pocket fees that the broker has to pay in order to get the transaction completed. Since they are not marked up, there is often no room for negotiation on them.

"If the broker is charging a loan-origination fee or points, these are typically the fees that can sometimes be negotiated. Because the mortgage brokerage company I work for is so large, they have very well established relationships with attorneys, appraisers, and title companies. Because we do such a large volume of business with these service providers, our fees for these services are typically quite low. We pass on that savings to our clients."

In preparation for the mortgage-application process, what type of paperwork should the borrower begin to gather?

Mark Giordani: "If you'll be using your income and assets to qualify and you're looking for the lowest rate mortgage possible, one of the best things you can do is collect your pay stubs for the past 30 days, obtain copies of W-2 forms for the past two years, if you're not self-employed, otherwise two years of tax returns will be required, and gather your bank statements that reflect the balances in your checking and savings accounts for the past two months.

You'll also want to provide two months' worth of statements for investment accounts and IRAs, for example. Two years of your employment and housing history is also typically a requirement.

"If you have potential challenges with your credit, income or employment, it's very tempting to sugar coat this information when explaining it to the broker. This is a mistake. The broker needs an accurate picture of your situation in order to get you the best possible deal. Anything you say that isn't accurate will be discovered later on when various documents are requested and reviewed. If the broker has you apply for a loan based on information you provide, but the documents don't support what you've said, your chances of having your application denied increase dramatically. Fortunately, there are, however, loan products available for almost any type of situation. It's important to obtain a loan you qualify for and one which you can ultimately afford. By providing accurate information, you'll save time, frustration and money by allowing the broker to fit you with a loan that's best suited to your situation.

"It is also important to know that, just because you are asked to document something, it is not necessarily because there is a problem. A mortgage decision can be a complicated one for a lender to make. Often they ask for proof of something, not because they doubt your word, but because they need to have it be part of your loan file for someone else in the process to see.

"The best time to discuss potential problems with your credit, income or employment is during the pre-qualification process, not once you're completing a formal application for a specific loan you might not actually qualify for. The documentation you supply must match the information you initially provide to the broker.

"Lastly, the temptation to fudge a loan application or parts of your income or employment history can be too strong for some borrowers. Banks have underwriting guidelines that they've spent millions of dollars to create. These guidelines are actually very lenient, but are based on the data from hundreds of thousands of loans that have gone bad in the past. If by telling the truth you can't get a loan, don't take the loan. You will be protecting yourself from a possible nightmare down the road. If you can't meet one of the flexible programs that are being offered, you may want to think twice before promising to pay back a loan you may not be able to afford. Banks are eager to loan you money. They make money by charging you interest. If they don't want to lend based on your circumstance, it is because they don't think they will get their money back. What would this mean to you? Foreclosure possibly ... and maybe worse."

What's the lowest credit score someone can have in order to qualify for a loan?

Mark Giordani: "This is a tricky question. There are so many different mortgage products available, someone with a credit score in the low 500s can potentially get approved for some type of loan, but the rate will be higher than for someone with a higher credit score. Different credit scores allow borrowers to qualify for different loan programs. As the risk increases for the lender, the rates and fees get higher. Your chances of approval and being able to get a more competitive rate increase greatly with a credit score over 620. To get the best rates and terms, a credit score in the 700s or 800s is most desirable."

Homebuyers Should Prequalify for a Mortgage

Now that you know how to choose a qualified, experienced, and knowledgeable mortgage broker or lender who is capable of guiding you through the mortgage-application-and-approval process or the refinancing process, the next chapter focuses on why you'd want to prequalify or get preapproved for a mortgage if you're shopping for a home. If your goal is to refinance your current mortgage, Chapters 5, 6, and 7 will be particularly helpful.

Forming Your Home-Buying Team

As you start the home buying process, in addition to hiring a mortgage broker or working directly with a lender, you'll need to tap the services of several professionals. Choosing the right people means obtaining the best guidance and information, which will save you time and money. The following list of experts is in alphabetical order, not in the order in which you'll need to hire them.

- Home appraiser—This professional helps to determine the current value of a home, based on a verity of criteria. The value of the home can be significantly different from the seller's asking price or the price that the buyer will ultimately pay.

- Home inspector—This professional carefully inspects the home prior to the purchase and provides a report on the condition of the home and any significant repair work that needs to be done.

- Insurance agent/broker—This specialist will help you define your home insurance needs and then sell you the appropriate policies to provide adequate coverage.

- Lender—This mortgage or finance company will provide you with the necessary funds (in the form of a mortgage) to purchase the home or refinance.

- Mortgage broker—This person acts as intermediary between you and the lender (such as a bank or financial institution), unless you deal with the lender directly. Mortgage brokers work with various lenders, so they can offer you the broadest range of mortgage products and help you choose the best one for your situation. Many mortgage brokers specialize in helping people with less-than-excellent credit get approved for some type of mortgage.

- Real estate agent or Realtor®—This professional will represent you, helping you find a home and then negotiate to purchase it. A real estate agent must be licensed and certified. A Realtor® has the same type of license, but is also a member in good standing of the National Association of Realtors®. He or she must adhere to an additional, strict code of ethics and conduct when doing business. The seller will also be represented by a real estate agent or Realtor®, who earns a commission based on the price paid for the home.

- Real estate attorney—This attorney specializes in real estate. Both you and the seller can benefit from hiring a real estate attorney due to the significant number of legal documents and legal proceedings involved with the purchase of a home.

- Seller—This is the person selling the home, its current owner. The seller may not belong on this list of experts, because he or she is not likely a real estate professional, but certainly is an expert on his or her home.

Depending on your situation, you may not have the need to work with each of the professionals on this list. For example, it's possible to find and negotiate to purchase a home without the help of a real estate agent and you could also potentially forgo a home inspection, but this is not advisable.

MORTGAGE

HELP

Prequalifying for a Mortgage

Now that you know how to find a mortgage broker or lender, the next step is to prequalify for a mortgage if you're buying a home or shop around for the best deals if you're refinancing. The next chapter focuses on the prequalification process for homebuyers. If you're looking to refinance, Chapters 5, 6, and 7 will help you choose the best mortgage product or loan to apply for through your mortgage broker or lender.

CHAPTER 4

Preparing for
a Mortgage

WHAT'S IN THIS CHAPTER

- Why prequalify?
- Prequalification vs. preapproval
- The prequalification process

There are many reasons to prequalify and obtain preapproval for a mortgage prior to finding a home and then making an offer. The most important reason is that this process will help you determine exactly how much you can afford. This will enable you to narrow your home search based on financial scenarios that makes sense for you.

When you begin searching for a home and potentially working with a real estate agent, some of the very first questions you'll need to answer are "Where would you like to live?" and "What type of home are you looking to purchase, in terms of size and features?" and "How much can you afford?" By prequalifying for a mortgage, you'll have a price range in mind that you know you can afford, before you start searching for the ideal home. Prequalifying also makes you more favorable to sellers, because they know right away you can afford their home and obtain the necessary financing.

MORTGAGE **If you already have a mortgage** and hope to refinance, you do not need to prequalify or get preapproved. To complete **HELP** the refinancing process, find a lender or mortgage broker, shop around for the best deal you qualify for, and then begin the mortgage-application-and-approval process. Details about refinancing can be found in Chapter 6.

When Buying a Home, Consider Prequalifying for a Mortgage

Several important factors go into determining how much you can afford for a new home, including the size of the mortgage you're qualified to obtain based on your credit history and credit score, income, savings, current debt, and employment. By prequalifying for a mortgage, you begin searching for a home knowing how much you can afford, based on the size of the mortgage you qualify for. Knowing this also allows you to easily calculate the down payment you'll need to make in order to afford the home you ultimately choose, based on the type of mortgage you'll be applying for.

Prequalifying for a mortgage will help determine where you can live and the size of your home, for example, plus save you the time of looking at properties you simply can't afford. You might want to move into a $375,000 home with a large front lawn and state-of-the-art appliances. However, you might qualify for only a $200,000 mortgage. If you can pay only $25,000 down, the maximum price of the home you should be searching for is $225,000, not $375,000. Knowing what you can afford will help you set parameters for your search.

Prequalifying for a mortgage also gives you greater negotiation leverage with sellers, especially if you're bidding against buyers who are not prequalified. If you prequalify, sellers know you potentially have the necessary funds available to purchase the home you're considering. The chances of your financing falling through are greatly reduced. This is important if the seller is looking to sell his or her home quickly and can't afford to waste time with potential buyers who are interested but don't have the finances available to purchase the home.

MORTGAGE **HELP** **The amount of the mortgage** for which you prequalify plus any money from savings, for example, you plan to use as a down payment establish the maximum you can spend on the home. It is not, however, the price you should agree to pay. Always negotiate with the seller for the lowest price possible. You don't need to spend the entire amount for which you're prequalified.

☆ ☆ **WARNING** ☆ ☆

Whatever the amount of the loan for which you prequalify, it's important to develop a realistic budget and determine, in advance, that you can afford to take on that mortgage and the expenses associated with it. Remember: becoming a homeowner requires more than just making your monthly mortgage payments on time. There are also taxes, insurance, possibly condo/homeowners' association fees, and home repair/maintenance expenses to consider. Make sure you'll be able to afford these ongoing expenses and have funds available for furniture, landscaping, new appliances, or any other home improvements you might want to make.

Prequalifying for a mortgage is an excellent strategy for home buyers. Even after you prequalify, you can still shop around for the best financing deals and continue to explore your mortgage options. Plus, before you begin searching for a home, you'll be able to determine if you need to take steps to improve the information on your credit report, such as correct inaccuracies or pay off credit card bills, in order to boost your credit score and qualify for better mortgage rates.

As you'll discover from this chapter, prequalifying for a mortgage is easy, whether you do it with a mortgage broker or lender on the telephone, in person, or even via the Internet.

Prequalification vs. Preapproval

When initially approaching a potential lender, it's important to understand the difference between being *prequalified* for a mortgage and being *preapproved*.

Prequalification is a fast, informal process. You provide the potential lender with basic financial information (without documenting it) and, based on that information, the lender will tell you approximately how much money you'd be eligible to borrow if you were to formally apply for a mortgage. You can use the prequalification process to determine what price range you can potentially afford for a home. The prequalification process can be done over the phone, in person, or online. It takes just a few minutes. However, it's not binding.

Preapproval requires the potential lender to gather financial information from you, evaluate your credit report and credit score, and review financial documents (such as tax returns, pay stubs, bank statements, and W-2 forms). If you meet the qualification requirements for the mortgage you're interested in, the lender will offer you a commitment to grant you the loan, provided that you continue to meet the same qualification requirements when you complete the full application.

Some lenders will put an expiration date on a preapproval. The preapproval process takes a bit longer and will require you to complete some forms and provide financial documentation, such as tax returns, bank statements, and pay stubs.

If you take on additional debt, such as a car loan, or lose your job after the preapproval but before the lender processes and approves your full mortgage application, there's a good chance your mortgage application will *not* be approved.

Make sure that when you begin working with a potential lender, you understand what you're being offered in terms of a prequalification or preapproval, how long it will remain in effect, and what limitations there are. Remember: everything you agree to should be put in writing.

The Prequalification Process

The prequalification process for a mortgage begins with questions that will be basically the same with any type of lender or broker. Based on the information you provide and your creditworthiness, the lender will be able to offer you mortgage options and help you choose one that you can afford and that will meet your needs.

Remember: in prequalifying for a mortgage, you are not completing the full mortgage application. This process simply gives you an idea of how much financing and the type(s) of mortgage product(s) you could obtain.

Mortgages and Refinancing: Get the Best Rates

Not all lenders offer the same mortgage products. Especially if your credit history is less than excellent, you'll definitely want to shop around, not just for the best rates, but for the type of mortgage that best meets your needs.

These are some of the prequalification questions a lender will ask you:

- What is your full name? What is your current address? What are your phone numbers?
- Will you have a co-borrower? If so, you'll need to provide the co-borrower's full name, current address, and phone number(s)
- What state are you looking to buy a home in?
- What type of property are you buying (single-family home, condo, etc.)?
- How will you be using your new property (as a primary residence, vacation home, etc.)?
- Are you a first-time buyer?
- What is your gross monthly income (before income taxes) and that of your co-borrower (your spouse, if applicable)? Your income should include your base pay, bonuses, commissions, tips, overtime, child support received (if any), retirement income (if any), annuity income (if any), alimony (if any), and any other money you receive or earn on a regular basis.
- Will you be documenting your income by providing tax returns, pay stubs, etc. or will you simply state your income, but not provide documentation?

- How much cash (from all sources, including savings, investments, gifts, and assets that can be converted into cash) do you have for your down payment and closing costs? Approximately what percentage of the purchase price does this down payment represent? (For some types of mortgages, a borrower must be able to make a 20-percent down payment to qualify. For other types of mortgages, such as an FHA mortgage, the down payment can be as low as three percent of the purchase price. Veterans who qualify for a VA loan may not need a down payment at all.)

MORTGAGE HELP **Your down payment must come** from savings, earned income, an inheritance, or a gift. It cannot be in whole or in part through loans.

- How would you define your credit history—excellent, good, average, or poor?
- What is your approximate credit score? (If you don't know this, the lender or broker will obtain your credit report and corresponding credit score from each credit bureau.)
- What are your current debts, including auto loans, student loans, credit cards, child support, alimony payments, other mortgages, etc.?
- What is your current employment situation (including length of employment, job title, etc.)?

Mortgages and Refinancing: Get the Best Rates

Based on the information you provide during the prequalification process, your *debt-to-income ratio* will be calculated (see Chapter 2). This is the amount of debt you have relative to your income. Many lenders specify a range for the debt ratio in order to qualify for their mortgage products. Fannie Mae, for example, follows the 28/38 rule, which means that to qualify for a Fannie Mae mortgage, you cannot spend more than 28 percent of your gross monthly income on housing or more than 38 percent of your gross monthly income on your monthly debt payments (that's the debt ratio), if your credit score is 620 or higher.

MORTGAGE

HELP

Based upon your income, an analysis of your debt, and your estimated down payment, your lender/broker will be able to calculate the maximum mortgage amount you could qualify for. This process is often called a *prequalification analysis*. It is meant to provide you with a rough idea of how much you could borrow. Once you provide the necessary information, including answers to the previous questions, the prequalification process should take just minutes. Be as accurate as possible, so the resulting figure is a realistic indication of what you can afford.

The prequalification analysis will generally remain valid for between 30 and 90 days, depending on the lender. Until you provide detailed information to the lender and complete a full application, however, it is not guaranteed that you'll be approved for the mortgage or that you will receive the interest rate being discussed.

The actual mortgage application process is much more time-consuming and in-depth than prequalifying for a mortgage. Completing a full mortgage application will require approximately an hour and require providing the lender/broker with financial documents, including tax returns, W-2s, pay stubs, and bank statements.

MORTGAGE HELP **There should be no cost or commitment** required when you begin working with a lender on a prequalification analysis. Based on the results of this analysis, the potential lender should be able to offer you a variety of mortgage products that you'd qualify for. However, if you choose to initiate the mortgage-application process, there will be a fee of several hundred dollars.

If you choose to pursue a preapproval (not just prequalification), you'll need to provide your Social Security number and that of any co-borrower and agree to allow the lender/broker to obtain your credit reports from the three credit bureaus.

MORTGAGE HELP **There are hundreds of mortgage products** out there, beyond the traditional 15-, 20-, and 30-year fixed-rate mortgages offered by banks. Each type of loan and each lender will have a different set of qualifications and approval guidelines. Even if you don't qualify for one type of mortgage, you may easily qualify for another. Work with one or more lenders/brokers to learn about all of the options available to you. If your credit history is below average, you may still qualify for a mortgage. However, the terms of that mortgage won't be as good as the terms offered to someone with excellent credit. Someone with below-average credit could wind up paying tens of thousands of dollars extra over the life of the mortgage.

Traditional banks are a lot tougher in their approval process than most other types of mortgage brokers and lenders. Unless you have excellent credit and an established relationship with a bank, you can often save a lot of money and be more easily approved for a mortgage if you shop around and approach mortgage brokers and lenders other than traditional lenders (such as banks).

Remember: a loan officer working for a mortgage broker is an intermediary between you and the lender(s) he or she represents. The mortgage broker is typically not the actual lender and does not make the final approval decision for the loan.

You're Prequalified—Now What?

Once you've found a mortgage broker, bank, financial institution, or lender to work with and you have a general idea of the type of mortgage you'd qualify for, you can begin searching for the perfect home.

It's easy to get confused or overwhelmed by all of the types of mortgage products out there. You'll also need to figure out how to obtain the best financing deal possible, find the perfect home, and negotiate the best purchase price with the seller. Since you're not a real estate expert, learn as much as you can from this book, but be sure to surround yourself with a lender/broker, a real estate agent, and a real estate attorney, people whom you trust and who can offer their guidance as you work your way through this entire process. Remember: it's OK to ask lots of questions and to check and recheck all of the information that's provided to you.

Never allow yourself to be tied to a mortgage or pushed into purchasing a home that you simply can't afford, even if you find a lender willing to approve you for the mortgage needed to purchase the home. It's your responsibility to calculate your budget and perform some financial calculations yourself to ensure that you're not taking on too much debt or overextending yourself financially in the short or long term. A mortgage is typically a 15-, 20-, or 30-year commitment. If you fail to meet that commitment down the road, you could end up facing foreclosure and/or be in serious debt.

Choosing the Best Kind of Loan

WHAT'S IN THIS CHAPTER

- The mortgage information you should know
- Learn about some of the many mortgage options
- More tips from mortgage consultant Mark Giordani

A s soon as you sit down with a mortgage broker, mortgage company, bank, credit union, savings and loan (S&L), other financial institution, or other lender, one of the first things you'll discover is that you have many options in choosing the best mortgage to meet your needs. This chapter focuses on finding the best mortgage. If you're looking to refinance, this chapter will be extremely helpful, but you'll also want to review Chapter 6 to discover additional options.

Choose the Right Mortgage Product to Meet Your Needs

Some of the considerations that should be taken into account as you choose the type of mortgage to apply for include:

- Your credit score and what information is on your credit reports
- Your ability to make a down payment
- The type of home you're purchasing
- Your current financial situation and ability to make the monthly mortgage payments and afford the real estate taxes, insurance, and other expenses
- Whether or not you can provide proof of employment, tax returns, pay stubs, bank statements, and other financial records to the lender
- How stable your current financial situation is. Do you anticipate a reduction in your income, or a change in your employment situation in the near future?

- How long you plan to live in the home you're interested in buying

As you read this chapter, it's important to remember that not all borrowers (home buyers) or homeowners looking to refinance will qualify for each type of mortgage. Some things to remember include:

- Some mortgage products are more suitable for people in specific financial or employment situations.
- Different mortgage brokers and lenders have different qualification requirements and approval guidelines for each of their mortgage products.
- Each broker or lender you meet with will offer a slightly different selection of mortgage product options, with brokers offering the largest selections of products because they typically represent a variety of different lenders.

☆ ☆ **WARNING** ☆ ☆

This chapter describes some of the most common mortgage options. However, as you begin working with brokers and lenders, you may be offered additional mortgage products or a variation on one of the common mortgage products described here. Before completing an application, make sure you understand the specific mortgage product you're applying for. Some of the things to look out for will be described within this chapter.

For each type of mortgage product described in this book, you'll read a brief description of how the mortgage works, plus learn about some of the pros and cons of each mortgage and the type of borrower it might appeal to. Because every home buyer or homeowner's situation is different, once you understand the basic information provided here, be sure to have a detailed discussion with your mortgage broker or lender about your specific options.

Virtually all of these mortgage products and options apply to home buyers and homeowners looking to refinance. For people refinancing their existing mortgage or who have purchased a home in the past, for example, additional mortgage products and other financing options may also be available.

MORTGAGE

HELP

Review the Truth-in-Lending (TIL), Good Faith Estimate (GFE), and HUD-1 statements provided by the lender or broker carefully before your closing. These documents will outline all of the fees you'll be paying that are associated with the loan. Because not all fees are listed on each document, it will be necessary to review and compare information on all three documents to get a clear picture of all fees and charges you're responsible for. Your real estate attorney is an excellent resource for guidance if you need information on any of these documents explained.

MORTGAGE

TERMS

Principal–The amount of money you initially borrow, not including interest, taxes or insurance premiums associated with the mortgage.

Mortgages and Refinancing: Get the Best Rates

Interest Rate—In relation to a mortgage, the interest rate represents the amount of interest charged on a monthly loan payment. It's usually expressed as a percentage.

APR (Annual Percentage Rate)—This is the annual (yearly) rate of interest that includes all fees and costs paid to acquire the loan (such as interest, mortgage insurance, certain closing costs, and points paid at closing). All lenders are obligated by law to disclose the APR. When comparing fixed-rate mortgages offered between multiple lenders/brokers, look at the APR, not just the interest rate or the monthly payment you'll be responsible to pay.

Lock—As the borrower, once you've selected the mortgage product you plan to apply for, because rates are always changing, it's an excellent strategy to lock in your rate with the lender or broker. A lock guarantees that the current rate you agree to will remain in effect for a predetermined period (30 days, for example), until you close your loan. Once your rate is locked, even if interest rates rise, you'll be protected. If interest rates go down, you could also typically qualify for this lower rate. A rate lock is not a loan approval.

Mortgage & Finance Calculation Software and Resources

Need help figuring out potential mortgage payments and creating an amortization table for a fixed rate loan? Can't figure out calculations associated with interest-only mortgages to see if this type of loan makes sense for you? What you need is a good financial calculator! You can find a

---

variety of different types of free loan calculators online at popular mortgage, personal finance, and loan-related web sites, including:

- A-Loan-Calculator.com: www.a-loan-calculator.com
- Bank of America Web site: www.bankofamerica.com/loansandhomes/index.cfm
- Bankrate.com: www.bankrate.com
- I-Mortgage-Rates.com: www.i-mortgage-rates.com/Mortgage-Calculator.aspx
- Mortgage101.com: www.mortgage101.com/Calculators/Index.asp
- Yahoo! Finance: http://finance.yahoo.com/loan/mortgage

You can also visit any consumer electronics store and pick up a hand-held financial calculator, like the Texas Instruments BA II Plus Financial Calculator (MSRP $30.99), or download mortgage/loan calculator software for your Palm-OS based PDA. LoanExpert Plus from Wakefield, LLC ($24.99, www.wakefieldsoft.com), for example, is a full-featured mortgage and loan calculator for Palm PDAs that easily handles loan amortization and interest-only loan calculations.

To find more online or software-based loan calculators, using any Internet search engine, such as Yahoo! or Google, use the search phrase 'mortgage calculator' or 'loan calculator.' Using any type of online or software-based loan or mortgage calculator can help you calculate interest, monthly payments, how much a loan could cost you, or how much you could save over the long-term.

Two of the worst mistakes someone can make as a homeowner is allowing his or her credit score to drop significantly and being late on the monthly mortgage payments. Either or both of these mistakes could keep you from refinancing your home or qualifying for a debt consolidation loan or HELOC that could help ease or fix a negative financial situation you experience in the future.

More Advice from Mortgage Consultant Mark Giordani

In this chapter, mortgage consultant Mark Giordani (see Chapter 3 for more information about him) offers additional advice for home buyers and homeowners looking to refinance. Later in this chapter, Giordani provides expert advice and information about specific mortgage products and loan options.

Based in Massachusetts, Giordani works with a broad range of clients from across America. He can be reached at (888) 695-3353 or (508) 291-8000.

After someone chooses their mortgage broker and begins working with them on the pre-qualification or actual application process, at what point should someone lock in their rate?

Mark Giordani: "Rates are constantly changing in the mortgage business. This is not something the mortgage broker controls. If you wait to lock in the terms of your loan, rates can stay the same, go up, or go down. Locking in your rate protects you for a pre-determined period of time and insures you'll get that rate, even if they go up. Make sure that the time period you lock in your rate for is long enough for you to complete the mortgage application process, find a home to purchase, handle your negotiations, and complete the closing process. If the duration of the lock isn't long enough, you'll wind up potentially having to pay for costly extensions. There's no harm in locking your rate early, as long as you know you may need to obtain an extension.

"A broker will charge anywhere from nothing to $500.00 to lock in a rate. In some cases, this lock in rate will also include the cost of the appraisal once you've selected a home. This fee is taken to cover the costs the mortgage broker will need to incur to pull your credit report and hire the appraiser, for example. In some cases, it is refundable. Rates locks are available for periods of up to one year, possibly longer, so you don't need to worry about getting the rate that's right for you.

"A reputable firm will actually reduce your rate during the lock period if the rate goes down between the time you locked and when your loan closes. Ask about the broker or lender's 'float-down' policy for details. A lock protects you from the rate going up, but if the rate goes down after you lock, you can often float-down and be protected from that. Just remember, you can't generally lock a rate until you have the property address of the property you plan to purchase. There are, however, one or two programs that let you lock and then find a property. A good broker can find you one."

How much of a time commitment is involved on the borrower's part to apply for and get approved for a mortgage?

Mark Giordani: "One of the frightening things for borrowers is that they don't know the answer to this question. The thing to understand is that this is a process and it takes time. A good mortgage broker should be able to explain to you what the process is up-front, and then be able to tell you what to expect during each step of the process based on your unique situation.

"How long the process takes will vary based on your situation and the type of mortgage product you're applying for. A lot also has to do with how quickly the borrower provides the necessary documentation needed to get their application approved. It's also important to understand that during this process, if you're asked for specific types of financial documents, this is a standard procedure. You are not being singled out. Different lenders require different documentation, based on the type of mortgage being applied for. The lender will often request additional documentation throughout the application and approval process."

What are some of the pitfalls a borrower should look out for early on when dealing with a mortgage broker?

Mark Giordani: "It's common for a borrower to call around and do some rate shopping. If you keep making enough calls, it's not uncommon to find a loan officer or broker who is going to either lie to you or who is incompetent. Without actually reviewing key financial information and documents that you provide, no mortgage broker can promise you an approval for any type of mortgage. If you pick up the phone and ask for a company's best rate on a 30-year, fixed-rate mortgage, they may quote you a very low and competitive rate, but that's not necessarily the rate you'll ultimately qualify for.

"Your best bet is to find an established and reputable broker who will then gather key financial information up-front so that they can provide you with the most accurate rate quote possible based on your qualifications. Otherwise, the quote they provide ultimately means nothing.

"While the Internet can he helpful in getting a mortgage, be careful. Clients that call me directly can most often get better pricing than they may have gotten if they came through to me via some of the popular loan shopping tools. This is because if they come directly to us, we don't have to pay fees and commissions to the lender search service they signed up for, and I can pass the savings directly to the consumer."

What is the biggest scam to watch out for when working with a mortgage broker?

Mark Giordani: "One of the biggest things to look out for is a broker who states you qualify for a mortgage at a very desirable rate without obtaining your pre-qualification information and reviewing your actual financial documentation first. A broker will need details about your credit, finances and employment before being able to provide even a ballpark figure as to what you qualify for. There is probably no lender that can accurately tell you what you will qualify for, if you're inquiring about a full documentation loan, that hasn't seen any of your documents, credit or employment history.

"As a general rule, anytime a deal seems too good to be true, it probably is. The mortgage business is a very competitive industry. If the price of gold is currently $300.00 per ounce, but someone is willing to sell it to you at $200.00 per ounce, there is probably a reason to be suspicious. The same is true with mortgages. If a broker offers you a significantly lower rate than other brokers, beware and make sure you understand all of the terms of that loan. Protect yourself by getting everything in writing and carefully reviewing your *good faith estimate and HUD-1 statement.*"

If someone is uncomfortable with the mortgage broker they begin working with, at what point can they walk away?

Mark Giordani: "A borrower can typically walk away at any point up until the closing. However, they run the risk of losing their deposit, appraisal fee and/or lock fee. You may be responsible for any out-of-pocket expenses the mortgage broker has incurred. Just because you can walk away from the loan transaction, you may not, however, be able to walk away from the Purchase and Sale Agreement you've signed with the seller. Before walking away, be sure to consult with your attorney, especially if a Purchase and Sale Agreement has already been signed.

"If you're participating in a refinance on your primary residence, you can cancel the transaction up to three business days after the closing by exercising your *Right of Rescission* [see Chapter 8]."

Prime versus Sub-Prime Loans: It's All About Your Credit History

Now that you know what's involved in working with a mortgage broker or lender to apply for a loan, the remainder of this chapter focuses on specific types of mortgage products. As you read about each type of mortgage product, Mark Giordani shares some insight about the pros and cons of each.

Borrowers with excellent credit and verifiable income often qualify for the best deals when it comes to mortgages. These borrowers qualify for the best terms and interest rates. These are considered "prime" or "A paper" loans. While many people might not qualify for a prime loan (for any number of reasons), there are a variety of sub-prime loans available. Many mortgage brokers and lenders specialize in catering to the needs of sub-prime borrowers. While a sub-prime borrower will typically pay a higher interest rate and higher fees to obtain a mortgage, actually getting approved is still a definite possibility.

> **Sub-Prime Borrower** and **Sub-Prime Lender**—A sub-prime borrower is someone who doesn't meet the approval guidelines for a prime rate mortgage. This could be due to a below-average credit score, a negative credit history, lack of employment information, the inability to provide various financial documents or verifiable income, or even a bankruptcy. A sub-prime lender is a lender or mortgage broker that specialized in working with sub-prime borrowers and that offers a variety of home financing options that have less strict or nontraditional approval guidelines.

15, 20, and 30-Year Fixed-Rate Mortgages

When you think of a mortgage, this is probably the most common and traditional type available. Not long ago, it was also the only type of mortgage product available and as a home buyer, you either qualified for it or you didn't. Today, with so many different mortgage products available from a wide range of financial institutions and lenders, this is no longer the case.

A fixed-rate mortgage is one where the interest rate does not change for the entire length of the mortgage. The longer the term of the mortgage, the lower your monthly payment will be, because your principal gets paid back over a longer period. The longer the length of the loan, however, the more interest you'll ultimately pay over the life of the loan, even though your monthly payments are lower. The higher your credit score, and the more you put down (and a few other factors), lthe lower your interest rate will be.

Take a look at the following example of a 15- and 30-year fixed-rate mortgage for a $200,000 loan, assuming a 7.5 percent interest rate.

Monthly Payment for a 15-Year Fixed-rate Mortgage: $1854.03

(Includes 180 monthly payments. Excludes taxes and insurance)

Total Interest Paid Over Life of Loan: $133,729.00

Monthly Payment for a 30-Year Fixed-rate Mortgage: $1398.43

(Includes 360 monthly payments. Excludes taxes and insurance)

Total Interest Paid Over Life of Loan: $303,425.00

As you can see, simply by extending the term of the loan, your monthly payment decreases, but the length of time it takes to pay off the loan increases as does the amount of interest you'd pay. Fixed-rate mortgages are typically available for a 10-, 15-, 20-, and 30-year term from most lenders. As always, you'll want to shop around for the best rates, terms, and options.

Once you start making monthly payments, you can track how much of your monthly loan payment is being applied to the principal versus interest using a simple amortization table or calculator.

> ### Words of Wisdom from Mortgage Consultant Mark Giordani
>
> "A fixed-rate mortgage is a great product if someone will be living in or owning the property for a long time. A fixed-rate mortgage is an amortized loan. Every month when you make your mortgage payment, some portion of it will go toward the principal and some to the interest. Historically, this has been a very popular loan choice, but has become less popular due to the variety of mortgage products now available."

Amortization—This is the repayment of a loan, such as a mortgage, where a portion of the payment is applied to the principal balance in addition to the interest owed. The more money that's applied to the principal over time, the lower the interest payment becomes, and the more equity the borrower builds in their property. When reviewing a potential fixed-rate mortgage option, print out an amortization table for the loan to see firsthand how your monthly payments will be applied to the loan's principal and interest from month to month throughout the duration of the loan. Using an amortization calculator, you can see that with a fixed-rate, 30-year mortgage at 7.5 percent interest, your monthly payment would be $1398.43 for the duration of the loan. For your very first payment, only $148.93 would be applied toward the principal, while $1250.00 would be applied to the interest payment. As you make your final payments almost 30 years later,

MORTGAGE TERMS

under $20.00 per payment would be applied toward interest with the rest going toward paying off the principal. You can find a free amortization calculator online at many real estate websites, including: www.bellemortgage.com/mort_calc1.htm.

Adjustable Rate Mortgage (ARM)

An adjustable rate mortgage (ARM) is one where the interest rate you pay from month to month during the life of the loan potentially changes. If the interest rate goes down, so does your monthly payment (in most cases). If the interest rate goes up, your monthly payment goes up. The benefit to this type of a loan is that initially, the interest rate you're offered could be significantly lower than what you'd be offered for a comparable fixed-rate mortgage. This makes becoming a homeowner more affordable (in terms of monthly payments) and often makes qualifying easier.

These loans are also referred to as "variable rate loans" and have been popular since the late 1980s. The big drawback to this type of a loan is that interest rates change constantly and you're basically gambling on the fact they'll go down, instead of up. Depending on the lender, you may not benefit, however, if rates go down, but you will be penalized if rates go up.

As you'll discover, there are mortgage products that start off as fixed-rate loans for the first few years, then automatically transform into an adjustable rate mortgage. This type of loan is good for someone with an average or below-average credit score, because you can qualify for a loan at a lower interest rate compared to a fixed-rate mortgage. During the one, two, three, or five year initial period, for example, when the rate is fixed, you can work toward improving your credit score. Then, before the loan transforms into an adjustable rate mortgage, you could refinance and potentially qualify for a fixed-rate mortgage at a more attractive rate (assuming interest rates don't go up considerably).

Some lenders offer "hybrid" or "convertible ARMs" that start off as adjustable rate mortgages and then can be transferred into a fixed-rate mortgage after a predefined period. Again, however, as the borrower, you are gambling on the fact that rates will stay the same or drop, not increase during the predefined period.

Because ARMs come in a variety of configurations, make sure you fully understand the mortgage product you're being offered. If the mortgage will start off as a fixed-rate mortgage and automatically transform into an ARM, you want to know exactly what the fixed-rate period will be, then how often the rate will adjust thereafter. Will the loan include pre-set caps to

---

☆ ☆ **WARNING** ☆ ☆

Before agreeing to an adjustable rate mortgage, consult with several lenders or mortgage brokers and determine what your monthly payments will be immediately and what they could be if rates increase. While the initial offer for this type of loan may be attractive, make sure it makes sense over the long term based on your personal financial situation.

---

maximize how high the interest rate can go once it becomes adjustable?

Words of Wisdom from Mortgage Consultant Mark Giordani

"When a bank is committing to a fixed interest rate for 10, 15, 20 or 30 years, there's a good chance that interest rates may rise, but the bank will not be able to pass that raise along to you. If a loan carries an adjustable interest rate, lenders are usually willing to offer a lower rate than they would for a fixed-rate mortgage. Because it's an adjustable rate, the lender can later raise the interest rate after one, two, three or five years (or sooner – be careful!), for example, based on the pre-determined guidelines of that loan. An ARM can save you money if it has a fixed-rate for several years and you know you don't plan to hang onto that property for that entire fixed-rate term.

"For example, if the ARM has a fixed-rate for the first five years, but you only plan to keep the home for four years, you can qualify for a lower interest rate for those four years and save money. The risk to you is that if you wind up keeping the property beyond the five years, your interest rate could go up, which means your monthly payment will increase. This can work the other way too. To your advantage, adjustable-rate mortgages can also adjust in a downward fashion."

Balloon Mortgage

A balloon mortgage has one final payment that is much higher than the regular monthly payment. Borrowers receive a lower rate and have lower monthly payments for a specific period of time, which can typically be between three and 10 years. After the predefined period, the borrower must pay off the principal balance in one lump sum. At this point, under certain circumstances, the loan could be converted to a fixed-rate or adjustable rate loan through refinancing. This type of mortgage product is best for people who plan to sell their home, pay it off, or refinance it *before* the balloon payment is ultimately due. It's potentially a good short-term loan option for people who qualify, because montly payments are typically significantly lower than other, more traditional types of loans. Homebuyers will benefit even more if the property appreciates (goes up) in value.

The drawback to this type of loan is that at the time the final balloon payment needs to be made, if you plan to refinance the loan to transform it into a fixed-rate mortgage, the interest rate could potentially be much higher than it was when you initially obtained the balloon loan.

Before utilizing any type of nontraditional loan, shop around for the best deal and consult with a financial planner and/or several lenders or mortgage brokers to insure you understand the specific terms you're being offered and that this type of loan is most suitable for your individual needs, based on your current financial and credit circumstances.

There are so many other products on the market, it is best to stay away from balloon loans, unless there is no other option and you fully undersand the extent of the risks involved.

Words of Wisdom from Mortgage Consultant Mark Giordani

"Balloon loans tend to have a lot of stigma attached to them. If you don't have the money for that final large payment, the lender could foreclose on the property. Generally speaking, if you can qualify for a non-balloon loan, I would pursue that option instead. Discuss your options with your mortgage broker or personal financial advisor."

Biweekly Mortgage (a.k.a Two-Step Mortgage)

A biweekly mortgage works just like a traditional fixed-rate mortgage, but instead of making regular monthly payments, you'd make lower biweekly payments (payments every two weeks). The benefit is that the loan will get paid off significantly faster than a standard fixed-rate loan, plus you'll wind up paying much less interest over the life of the loan. You'll also be building up equity in your home much faster using this type of loan and could cut the time it takes to pay it off by up to eight years.

Often, the biweekly payments will automatically be deducted from your checking account by the lender. The main drawback to this type of loan is that you must be able to afford to make the payments every two weeks. Your ability to do this will most likely be impacted by how you're paid at your job.

Basically, what would be your monthly payment for a fixed-rate mortgage divided in half, with smaller payments due every two weeks? Let's use the example of a 30-year, $200,000 fixed-rate mortgage with a 7.5 percent interest rate. By transforming this loan into a biweekly mortgage, instead of paying approximately $303,425 in interest over the life of the loan, you'd pay only about $225,321 in interest. This represents a savings of over $78,104. You'd also pay off the loan 6.5 years sooner (in 23.5 years as opposed to 30 years). In this situation, your biweekly mortgage payment would be about $699.21 (excluding taxes and insurance).

For those who can afford to make the biweekly payments, this can be a very attractive opportunity. Another option is to accept a standard fixed-rate loan that has no prepayment penalties and to make one or more additional payments toward principal each year. This too will make paying off the loan faster and save you a fortune in interest over time.

Some companies refer to biweekly mortgage products as "mortgage savings programs." The qualifications are basically the same for this type of loan versus a fixed-rate mortgage.

MORTGAGE

HELP

Words of Wisdom from Mortgage Consultant Mark Giordani

"A biweekly mortgage isn't much different than any other mortgage, except that the payments are made more often than once per month. What it boils down to is that if a mortgage payment is made biweekly, that's 26 payments per year, which equates to making 13 monthly payments per year instead of 12. I would not recommend paying extra for a biweekly payment privilege. If a broker or lender is going to charge you extra, consider accepting a traditional fixed-rate mortgage and then making one or more extra payments toward the loan's principal per year on your own. The result in terms of your savings will be basically the same and you will have control over when and whether or not to send in those extra payments."

More Mortgage Options For People with Less Than Perfect Credit

There are a wide range of mortgage options designed for people who have a credit history that's less than perfect or who don't have easily verifiable income. These people wouldn't typically qualify for a traditional, fixed-rate mortgage from a local bank or financial institution.

These mortgage options relate directly to what's required for loan approval and can be applied to a variety of mortgage products, although they're typically used for fixed-rate or adjustable rate mortgages. As you'll discover, what's required to qualify for each will vary greatly by loan product and lender. These loans could have higher costs and a higher interest rate associated with them, compared to a fixed-rate mortgage offered to someone with an excellent credit score. Be sure to discuss these options with your mortgage broker if you believe you could benefit from one of them based on your personal financial situation. Some of these options are referred to as *sub-prime, non-conventional* or *Alt-A* loans.

Stated Income / Stated Asset Mortgages—To qualify you for a mortgage, the lender will rely on financial information that you state is accurate, but this information will not have to be verified using tax returns, pay stubs, or bank statements, for example.

MORTGAGE TERMS

> ### Words of Wisdom from Mortgage Consultant Mark Giordani
>
> "This type of loan is available to certain qualified borrowers on specific loan scenarios. The borrower does not need to provide any supporting documentation about their income or assets. The borrower literally just states what their income and assets are to the lender. This requires you to make a declaration to the lender that the information you're providing is totally accurate. Depending on your employment situation, requirements for this type of loan will vary. Keep in mind, a lender will verify your employment. If you

state you're earning a specific salary for doing a specific job, the lender will also do research to make sure that the income you're declaring is within a reasonable and realistic range. Depending on the loan-to-value calculation and your credit situation, many lenders won't charge extra for this type of loan, nor will you have to pay a higher rate. A SISA (Stated Income / Stated Asset) loan can be a real timesaver."

MORTGAGE **No Income Verification Loans**—To qualify for this type of mortgage product, the borrower will not need to provide proof of their income.
TERMS

Words of Wisdom from Mortgage Consultant Mark Giordani

"This type of loan allows the borrower to potentially obtain a loan without having to state their income or prove their income. The approval decision is based primarily on assets owned and the borrower's credit. There are several different categories of no income verification loans. Again, as the risk for the lender increases, the rate the borrower will need to pay increases. These days, it is possible to obtain a mortgage without having to prove your income, assets or employment, as long as you have qualifying credit."

MORTGAGE **No Documentation Mortgages**—To qualify for this loan, the borrower will need to have a qualifying credit history; how-
TERMS

ever, they will not have to provide proof of income, assets, or employment in conjunction with their mortgage application.

Words of Wisdom from Mortgage Consultant Mark Giordani

"A lot of people assume that with this type of loan, there is no paperwork involved. That's not the case. There is still an application that needs to be completed. You will still need to provide your name, address, date of birth, Social Security number and credit information. You will not, however, have to provide any information whatsoever, about your assets, employment or income. You may need to provide information about your current housing situation and how much you pay for rent. This may be verified later by the lender. A no documentation loan means you don't need to supply a lot of supporting documents, like bank statements or pay stubs. There is still, however, a lot of paperwork involved with this type of loan during the closing itself.

"This type of loan is ideal for people who have privacy concerns and don't want to reveal certain information about their finances. For someone with poor credit and who desires a no documentation loan, there's an entirely separate category of loans referred to as *Hard Money Loans*. Hard money lenders primarily look at collateral or the value of the property, not at someone's credit or character. This type of lender typically won't

---

lend more than 65 percent of the property's value. You'll also be required to pay a significantly higher interest rate and other fees.

MORTGAGE **No Down Payment Loans—**For people who qualify, there are a variety of mortgage products that require either a very small **TERMS** or no down payment.

Words of Wisdom from Mortgage Consultant Mark Giordani

"A no down payment loan is one that requires absolutely no down payment. This is a 100 percent financed transaction, which has become extremely common these days. There are also loan programs that allow the borrower to receive a financial gift from a relative, for example, to cover their down payment. FHA loans and VA loans typically require little or no down payment. There are many loans that require only $500 of the borrower's own funds to use toward the home purchase. There are even loan programs that will provide the buyer with 103% of the property value to help cover closings costs and other fees.

"On loans with no down payment or a down payment that's below 20% of the purchase price of the home, expect in some circumstances, you will be asked to pay for insurance for the lender in case the loan goes bad. This insurance is known as PMI or Private Mortgage Insurance.

There are many ways to get around this insurance requirement. Find a broker who is an expert in this area and you may be able to save some significant money."

***Private Mortgage Insurance (PMI)*–**For borrowers applying for a conventional mortgage, but who don't have a 20 percent down payment, they're typically required to purchase *Private Mortgage Insurance*, which is an insurance policy that guarantees the lender will be paid, even if the borrower defaults on the loan. The cost of this insurance is paid for by the borrower and is added to the monthly mortgage payment. The lower the down payment the borrower provides, the higher the cost of this insurance. Once the borrower owns at least a 20 percent equity in their home, this insurance can be cancelled and the mortgage can be adjusted accordingly.

FHA Loans

The FHA (Federal Housing Administration) offers government-insured loans that allow people to purchase property with low down payment requirements. While the FHA is not a lender unto itself, it encourages lenders to offer loans to people who would otherwise not meet mortgage qualification requirements by guaranteeing the lender will be repaid, even if the borrower defaults. This is done by requiring the borrower to purchase special mortgage insurance (referred to as *Mortgage Insurance Premiums* or *MIP*). An estimate for the monthly cost of this added (required) insurance can be calculated by multiplying the loan amount by .5, then dividing that number by 12. These MIP insurance fees typically last for about seven years. MIP is similar to Private Mortgage Insurance (PMI), which is required for other types of loans.

Initially, FHA home loans were for first-time home buyers; however, they're not only for this purpose. Instead of requiring a 20 percent down payment, an FHA loan requires a down payment of three percent (3%) of the purchase price, which for many people is much more affordable because the initial cash required to close the loan is lower.

Keep in mind, there are pre-set loan limits for FHA loans, which vary by region. To learn more, visit the FHA's web site at www.hud.org, or discuss this option with your mortgage broker.

Words of Wisdom from Mortgage Consultant Mark Giordani

"FHA loans are being insured by the Federal Housing Administration. Because the government is willing to bear some of the risk for the loans, lenders are willing to offer easier credit and income qualifications. These tend to be a little more complex and lengthier to apply for, because a number of government forms also need to be completed. Depending on the circumstances, this type of loan can save borrowers money. In other situations, however, the loan limits may not be high enough to cover the purchase

---

price of a home in certain geographic areas. A good mortgage broker will be able to help you determine if an FHA loan would be a better alternative than another type of loan and step you through the process."

Interest-Only Mortgage

In recent years, this has become a popular mortgage product among homebuyers, because it allows people to purchase a more expensive home without dramatically increasing their monthly payments. This type of loan is more suitable for people who expect their income to increase significantly in the future, or who expect the value of their property to increase significantly over time.

As the name of this mortgage product suggests, the monthly payment the borrow makes represents only the interest due on the loan. No portion of the principal gets paid back each month. Thus, unless the property increases in value, no equity is ever built up. If the value of the property decreases before it's sold, the borrower could wind up owing money.

For this type of loan, a five or ten year interest-only period is standard. After this period, the principal balance is then amortized for the remaining term of the loan. Thus, if a borrower had a 30-year mortgage, but the first 10 years were interest-only, at the end of the initial 10-year period, the principal balance would be amortized for the remaining period of 20 years. For a borrower who expects their income will increase, this enables him/her to initally borrow more than they could otherwise afford at the time of the purchase, because monthly payments are lower compared to a typical fixed-rate mortgage

Like all non-traditional mortgage products, this one has pros and cons which you should review with a financial planner or broker. Interest-only loans are not suitable for everyone.

MORTGAGE **One common trend is for lenders** to offer an option where borrowers can obtain a more traditional type of loan; how-**HELP** ever, during months when money is tight, they can make interest-only payments instead of their full monthly payment due on the mortgage. This gives homeowners an extra level of financial flexibility and the ability to better manage periodic unexpected expenses.

Words of Wisdom from Mortgage Consultant Mark Giordani

"Interest-only loans are a relatively new mortgage product. For the right borrower, they can be ideal. An interest-only loan has the potential to be riskier than other types of mortgages, but it also has many advantages that you should discuss with your broker.

"This type of loan can be excellent if real estate prices are on the rise, because even though you're not building up equity in the home based on your monthly payments, you are building up equity if the value of the property increases. This type of loan is excellent for someone who doesn't have

---

a steady income, who has a seasonal income, or who tends to be paid through on commissions. With this type of loan, the borrower always has the option to pay toward the principal of the loan and build equity at anytime.

"If you utilize this type of loan, make sure you fully understand the terms. Interest-only loans are often associated with ARMs, as opposed to fixed-rate mortgages. There are, however, fixed-rate loans available that have an interest-only option, but expect to pay more in interest for this feature.

"One other advantage of an interest-only loan is something called 'recasting.'

If you take out a $200,000 fixed-rate loan, your monthly payment stays the same for the life of the loan – whether or not you pay any extra toward the principal balance.

"With an interest-only loan, one nice feature is that if you are able to pay down the principal balance in an accelerated way, your monthly payments will reflect those payments, in most cases, right away. So, as you are paying it down, your payments get lower. This can be a great feature for lots of borrowers who get their income in large payments or bonuses. With all loans, especially interest-only loans and ARM's, you must make every effort to understand what you are getting.

"If you take out a five year interest-only loan, for example, your rate and payments would be fixed for five years.

After the fifth year, however, your payment could go up if interest rates go up. Also, the entire principal balance of the loan will now have to be paid off over a 25 year payment schedule. This can mean sharp increases in the payments you need to make just a few years down the road.

"I would also suggest that borrowers exercise caution with a new category of loans, called 'Option Loans,' 'Pay Option Arms,' or 'Pick a Payment Loans.' These loans traditionally offer three or four different monthly payment option scenarios. If used irresponsibly, they can result in losing equity in your home. If you are offered a loan that features multiple payment options, including one payment option that doesn't even cover the monthly interest due, investigate fully."

VA Loans

The Veterans Administration (VA) offers mortgage opportunities to veterans of the U.S. military. This program has been in effect since 1944 and allows qualified borrowers to purchase a home with no down payment whatsoever. In other words, 100 percent financing is made available through this program. VA Loans are available to enlisted service personnel with continuous service for a predetermined number of days (based on when the enlisted person served), veterans with honorable discharges, and to surviving spouses of enlisted soldiers killed in the line of duty. Some Reservists also qualify. The amount that can be borrowed varies by region. These loans only apply to single or multi-family home purchases that will be owner-occupied. The majority of VA loans are 15- or 30-year, fixed-rate mortgages.

For additional information about VA loans, speak with a mortgage broker who specializes in this type of home financing option, or visit the VA web site at www.homeloans.va.gov.

Words of Wisdom from Mortgage Consultant Mark Giordani

"Some VA loans are offered at very good rates and terms. They offer an excellent opportunity for veteran borrowers. The thing about VA loans is that there are not as many different mortgage product types available. In some cases, a non-VA loan may be better suited for a borrower. VA loans require extra paperwork and often take longer to process and get approved than other types of loans."

Assumable Loans

This is a mortgage that can be transferred from someone else, such as the person from whom you're buying your home (the seller). This means that the person taking over the loan assumes the liability for it and becomes responsible for making the monthly payments. This can be attractive if the person you're buying the home from has a very low interest rate associated with the loan that you could not necessarily qualify for yourself. If you take over the seller's mortgage (assume their loan), you will be responsible to pay the difference between the remaining balance owed on the loan and the asking price (or negotiated selling price) of the home. This difference would need to be made as a down payment.

Only mortgages that have an "assumption clause" included within them can be assumed by another party. In most cases, ARM loans are assumable, while fixed-rate loans are not.

Words of Wisdom from Mortgage Consultant Mark Giordani

"Assumable loans aren't really an entirely separate type of loan, but are more of a feature that some loans include. The advantage is that if you sell the home, a new, qualified buyer may be able to take over the loan without having to refinance it. If an assumable loan is something that is extremely important to you, make sure the terms of the assumability are in writing and are exactly what you anticipated."

Some Pointers on Points

When it comes to mortgages, one point is equal to one percent of the mortgage amount. For a $100,000 loan, for example, one point would be equal to $1,000. In order to reduce the interest rate offered on a loan, borrowers can often pay points on the loan at the closing. Points paid to

---

reduce your interest rate are referred to as "discount points." A one point loan, for example, will have a lower interest rate than a zero point loan. By paying points, you're making a tradeoff between paying money at the closing versus paying money (in the form of interest) later. The money you pay for points is in addition to your down payment (not part of it).

Deciding whether or not to pay points on a loan should be determined in part by how long you plan to keep the property, and whether or not you can recoup the amount you pay in points if you plan to sell the property or refinance the loan within several years. As a general rule, it doesn't make sense to pay points on a loan if you plan on keeping that loan for less than four years.

Because lenders allow you to choose amongst a variety of rate and point combinations for the same loan product, the Mortgage101.com web site (www.mortgage101.com) recommends, "When comparing rates from different lenders, make sure you compare the associated points and rate combinations of the offered program. The published Annual Percentage Rate (APR) is a tool used to compare different terms, offered rates, and points among different lenders and programs."

It's important to note that some lenders charge points as part of their loan origination fee.

MORTGAGE TERMS ***Mortgage Banker*—**There are many types of lenders (also referred to as *mortgagees*) who offer mortgages, such as a bank, credit union, or savings and loan. Another type of lender is a mortgage banker. This is a company or individual who uses their own funds to lend money. Many mortgage bankers have their own mortgage approval guidelines and requirements, which may be more flexible or lenient than a traditional bank, for example. Mortgage brokers typically represent a handful of mortgage bankers and other types of lenders.

MORTGAGE HELP **Confused about the lingo** used to describe various mortgage products? You're certainly not alone! Check out the mortgage glossary at the end of this book or the online glossary found at the HUD web site (www.hud. gov/offices/hsg/sfh/ buying/glossary.cfm). The Yahoo! Real Estate Glossary (http://realestate. yahoo.com/loans/glossary.html) is also a useful resource for decoding mortgage lingo.

Refinancing Made Simple

While refinancing involves many of the same steps as obtaining a first mortgage, the process can be somewhat easier, in part because as the borrower, you've been through the process before and know what to expect. What you might not realize, however, is that when refinancing, you also have many options pertaining to the type of mortgage product you utilize.

As you'll discover, it's extremely important to understand the mortgage product you decide to apply for. It's equally important, however, to make sure that the mortgage product makes sense for you, based on your objectives, how long you plan to remain in the home, and your unique financial situation. Be sure to crunch the numbers to insure that by refinancing you'll actually be achieving the desired goals. The next chapter focuses on refinancing.

All About
Refinancing

Mortgages and Refinancing: Get the Best Rates

As a homeowner, chances are you've gone through the process of applying for a mortgage, getting approved, and participating in a closing, three of the major steps that lead to home ownership. The rate and terms of the mortgage you obtained to purchase your home were based on your financial situation, the information on your credit reports, your credit score, your employment situation, your income, and the interest rates being offered at the time.

Whether you obtained that mortgage six months ago, several years ago, or more than one or two decades ago, chances are things have changed in your financial and credit situation and in interest rates and mortgage products now available. For any number of reasons, many of which will be described in this chapter, it might make sense for you to consider refinancing your mortgage.

☆ ☆ WARNING ☆ ☆

Don't get caught up in the advertising hype about refinancing deals that sound good but don't make financial sense for you! Before refinancing, make sure you understand exactly how you will be benefiting from the process, how much you will save over the life of the loan, how long it will take you to recoup the expenses of refinancing, and how much you will pay in costs and fees. You also want to know what your out-of-pocket expenses will be prior to and at the closing.

Refinancing 101

Refinancing is the process of replacing a mortgage on a property with another mortgage with different terms. Despite the time and effort it takes to find a lender or broker, shop around for the best deal, choose a mortgage product, complete the mortgage application process, provide the necessary paperwork and forms to the lender, and participate in the closing, there are many reasons why you might want to refinance now or in the future. In fact, between the time you buy your home and either sell it or pay off the mortgage, you might opt to refinance more than once as situations change.

In order to refinance, you'll need to qualify all over again and go through virtually the same mortgage-application process as the first time. You can dramatically improve your chances of getting a lower interest rate and better terms on your new mortgage if:

- You credit score has improved since you obtained your mortgage.
- You can show that you've made all of your monthly mortgage payments on time.
- Your income has increased since you obtained your mortgage
- You've built up equity in your home.
- You plan to refinance a lower principal.
- You can reduce the costs of refinancing, which is easier if you have excellent credit.

Mortgages and Refinancing: Get the Best Rates

There are ways to save money when you refinance, if you take the time to crunch the numbers, fully understand the terms of the new loan, consider the costs associated with refinancing, and then shop around for the very best deal you qualify for. No matter what type of mortgage you have now, your monthly payment is determined primarily by the following factors:

- The principal
- The interest rate
- The length
- The terms
- Fees you paid in conjunction with the loan, including closing costs

Often when you refinance, the closing costs and most other fees associated with refinancing can be built into the new loan to avoid out-of-pocket expenses at the closing. You will often, however, need to pay for the appraisal in advance. For a typical single-family home, an appraisal will cost between $250 and $350, depending on your geographic area.

MORTGAGE HELP

When you consider refinancing, if you can change one or more of the above factors in your favor, such as lowering your interest rate, you could potentially lower your monthly payment and/or save on interest over the life of the loan. Whether you decrease your principal, get a lower interest rate, or change your loan duration, the smallest reductions result in significant savings over the life of the loan.

MORTGAGE HELP **You may hear from friends** or co-workers around the water cooler that it's important to wait for interest rates to drop by at least two percent before you refinance if you hope to save money. This isn't necessarily so. Instead, focus on what the potential new loan offers, the costs associated with it, and how long it'll take to break even, compared with how long you plan to keep the home. Every situation is different. Refinance only if it makes financial sense and you're able to achieve your goals.

As you consider your refinancing options, think carefully about your goals. What are you trying to do? Lower your monthly payment? Shorten the term of the loan? Cash out on the equity in your home? If your current financial situation is very strong, you might want to use your good credit, the equity in your home, and your current income, to invest in additional real estate. If, however, times are tough financially, you could refinance in order to obtain some cash. When crunching the numbers to see if refinancing makes sense, knowing how long you intend to own the property can also become a factor, especially if you'll be dealing with an adjustable-rate mortgage. But more on that later.

Depending on what you're trying to accomplish and your ability to qualify for approval, your refinancing options will vary greatly. Knowing your goals will help you and your lender/mortgage broker determine your best options.

☆ ☆ **WARNING** ☆ ☆

Calculate all of the additional fees and closing costs associated with refinancing and then calculate how long it will take you to break even and start saving money. If your plan is to sell or refinance again in just a few months or years, refinancing might not save you money.

As you shop for the best refinancing deals, determine whether any of the mortgage products available could potentially save you more money. For example, you could go from one fixed-rate loan to another, or go from a fixed-rate loan to an adjustable-rate loan, or switch to some other type of mortgage product. In addition to the information in this chapter, be sure to read Chapters 5 and 7 for other loan options if you're looking to refinance or cash out on the equity in your home.

Rescission period–If you're refinancing for your primary residence, there's a mandatory period of three days (excluding Sundays and holidays) after the closing in which you can change your mind and pull out of the deal with no strings attached. For this reason, if you're receiving cash as part of your refinancing, you'll have to wait three days, so plan accordingly. Likewise, the new lender will not fund the new loan (pay off your current loan) until after the third day. During this time, review all of the paperwork once again and make sure it's accurate and acceptable and you're comfortable with the terms of

MORTGAGE TERMS

the new mortgage. If you choose to pull out within the rescission period, you need to fill out the appropriate paperwork (supplied at your closing) and follow the procedure, which will be explained at the closing.

Watch out for Prepayment Penalties

By paying off the loan early, the borrower saves money in interest—which would be income for the lender. So, some lenders build prepayment penalties into their mortgages in order to deter the borrower from refinancing or paying off the debt before the term ends.

If your mortgage has a prepayment penalty and you choose to refinance, you could be charged extra to do so. When shopping for a mortgage, look for products that contain absolutely no prepayment penalty. Some loans have a prepayment penalty for only the first few years of the loan. If possible, avoid these too. You never know when your financial situation or interest rates will change dramatically, enabling you to refinance at a better rate and with more attractive terms. If your loan has no prepayment penalty, you have more options.

MORTGAGE HELP   **Not all prepayment penalties** are created equal! Just because a loan has a prepayment penalty, that doesn't mean you should necessarily walk away. Discuss with your broker or lender the specifics of any prepayment penalty.

MORTGAGE TERMS   *Prepayment penalty*—This is a fee a lender can charge the borrower for paying off the loan before the end of the term. The lender uses the penalty as an incentive against refinancing.

Popular Reasons for Refinancing

There are many reasons why homeowners refinance. Your reason(s) will help determine which mortgage products you apply for and best suit your needs. Once again, it's important to sit down with several lenders or mortgage brokers in order to review your current situation and determine what options are available to you for refinancing or cashing out on the equity in your home. If there are any additional expenses, such as closing costs or a cash-out, the refi is called an *equity take-out* or *cash-out refinance.*

Here's some information about some of the most popular reasons why homeowners choose to refinance.

Obtain a Lower Interest Rate

Interest rates offered by lenders change daily. The rate you received when you were approved for your current mortgage was based on a variety of factors. If interest rates have gone down in general, even by a fraction of a point, it might make sense to refinance in order to reduce your monthly payment and the interest you'll be paying over the life of the loan.

Here's an example. If you have a $200,000, 30-year, fixed-rate mortgage at 7.25 percent, your monthly payment is $1,364.35 and the interest over the 30 years is $291,166.

If interest rates drop to 6.75 percent, for the same $200,000 30-year, fixed-rate mortgage, your monthly payment would be $1,297.20 and the interest you'd pay would be $266,992. So, not only would your monthly payment drop by $67.15 per month, you'd save $24,174 in interest. But wait, there's more! If you've already been paying off your original mortgage on time for five years, for example, your outstanding principal would be lower than the $200,000 you borrowed. You could now refinance that lower amount for either a full 30 years (which would lower your payment even more) or only 25 years (or less). So, you could save in interest plus cut the term of your mortgage.

Use an amortization calculator, like the one at finance.realtor.com/HomeFinance/calculators/mortgagepayment.asp, to calculate the financial benefits of refinancing a fixed-rate mortgage. You can also find online calculators that'll help you determine if refinancing with another type of loan makes more financial sense in your situation. Ideally, however, you should talk with at least one mortgage broker or lender who can review your refinancing options based on current interest rates.

Even if interest rates in general have not dropped, you can still refinance and benefit from a lower interest rate in one of several ways. First, if your credit score has improved since you obtained your mortgage, chances are you'd now qualify for a lower interest rate, especially if you've built up equity in your home and you've made all of your mortgage payments on time. Second, if you refinance you can pay points to lower your interest rate. Third, you could potentially switch from a fixed-rate mortgage to an adjustable-rate mortgage that offers lower rates and better terms. If there's a way to decrease your interest rate, even by a fraction of a point, the benefits of refinancing could be dramatic.

Get Better Terms on the Mortgage

When refinancing, you can adjust the terms of your mortgage or potentially save money by switching mortgage products altogether. You could go from a fixed-rate mortgage to some type of adjustable-rate mortgage or an interest-only mortgage, for example.

By switching to an adjustable-rate mortgage (with an initial fixed-rate period), you could probably get a more attractive interest rate, which would save you money. You'd run the risk, however, that after the fixed-rate period your interest rate could rise significantly. You could possibly avoid this increase by refinancing again down the road, but you could lose out over the long term if interest rates rise significantly or you have to pay high closing costs each time. Before choosing this refinancing option, consider how long you'll be in your home. If you know you'll be moving in four years, for example, you can refinance now with an ARM that has a fixed-rate period of five years and benefit from the savings with no risk of a higher rate after that period, because you'll be moving or selling the home. Of course, consult with your lender or broker to see if this scenario works for you.

Different mortgage products and different lenders/brokers offer vastly different terms, which is why it's important to evaluate your needs and shop around for the best deal. If you want to save money by refinancing, even a subtle change in the interest rate, the duration, or the terms could make a significant difference.

MORTGAGE HELP

MORTGAGE **HELP** **When comparing totally different** mortgage products, you must evaluate more than just the interest rate, duration, terms, and fees to determine which deal would be the best option for what you're trying to accomplish. Use a financial calculator to calculate how your situation would benefit from each scenario. Unfortunately, if you're evaluating different loan types, comparing the APRs (annual percentage rates) won't do you much good. The APR represents your cost to borrow money, but to compare mortgage products objectively by APRs, the loan products must be similar.

Shorten or Lengthen the Duration of the Mortgage

Whether or not you can qualify for a lower interest rate, you can still benefit financially if you can refinance at better terms. One way to do this is to refinance for a shorter period. If you go from a 30-year fixed-rate loan to a 25-year or 20-year fixed-rate loan, your savings in interest over the life of the loan will be dramatic. If you can get a lower rate when you reduce the length of the mortgage, you could potentially decrease your monthly payment as well.

For example, if you started with a 20-year fixed-rate mortgage and have been paying it off for ten years, you could now refinance at the same or even a higher interest rate, but set the length of the new loan back to 20 or more years. This would *not* save you money (in fact, it would cost you more), but it would lower your monthly payment, which might help you address current financial shortfalls or problems.

Cash out on the Equity in Your Home

If you made a down payment on your home when purchasing it, that amount immediately established equity. Since then, if you've been paying off a small portion of your mortgage principal with each monthly payment, you've been slowly building equity. Finally, if the appraised value of your home has increased since you purchased it, the difference between its current value and your purchase price also represents equity in your home.

Regardless of what mortgage product you use to refinance, the lender will almost always require you to maintain at least some equity in your home (at least ten to 25 percent). However, there are exceptions. There are some refinancing options that allow you to refinance for more than 100 percent of the home's appraised value, but you must have excellent credit and meet other requirements to obtain this type of loan.

MORTGAGE HELP

As long as you have equity in your home and meet the loan qualification guidelines of the lenders, you can borrow against or cash out on your equity in order to obtain cash. Doing this would increase the amount you owe on your mortgage (or other types of loans, such as a home equity line of credit), but you could access cash quickly.

Here are some of the most popular reasons why people opt to cash out on some or all of their equity:

- Make home improvements
- Pay for school or college tuition

- Consolidate and pay off high-interest debt, such as credit cards
- Finance a divorce settlement
- Pay medical expenses not covered by health insurance
- Purchase a big-ticket item, such as an expensive car or boat
- Invest in another property, such as a vacation home or investment property

MORTGAGE

HELP

Typically, tapping the equity in your home for a significant amount of money is ultimately cheaper than using a high-interest credit card or taking out some other type of loan. Plus, there are certain tax advantages, since the interest you pay on your home loan is tax-deductible, while the interest you pay on other types of unsecured loans is not deductible.

In some rare situations, instead of refinancing your mortgage, the lender will allow you to modify your loan. *Loan modification* is most common when the borrower wants to keep all of the terms of the loan identical, but can now put a large sum of money toward the principal, which will lower the monthly payments.

When you decide to refinance in order to cash out on your equity, your options will depend on your credit history and your ability to meet the eligibility and approval requirements of the various lenders and brokers. Aside from refinancing, Chapter 7 explores second mortgages, home equity loans, and home equity lines of credit (HELOC) as potential options if you wish to tap into your equity.

The Paperwork You'll Need to Refinance

Once you decide to refinance, you'll want to gather pertinent information about your current mortgage and financial situation. This includes reacquainting yourself with the terms of your mortgage. As you start talking to lenders and brokers about refinancing, early on in the application process you'll need to provide the following information, in addition to the information you'd need to provide if you were buying a home and shopping for a mortgage:

- The current value of your home (an appraisal will be ordered by the lender or broker)
- The current amount owed on your mortgage
- The interest rate and terms of the current mortgage
- Your credit history and credit score (the broker or lender will order copies of your credit reports and obtain your credit scores)

During the refinancing application process, be prepared to provide the lender or broker with your pay stubs from the last 30 days, copies of W-2 forms for the past two years (or tax returns for the same period, depending on your employment situation), two months' worth of bank statements, two months' worth of statements for your investment and IRA accounts, and information about your employment and housing for the past two years. You'll also need to provide copies of your current mortgage documents (which you received at the closing). To save time and avoid unnecessary delays, start gathering these documents early in the refinancing process.

Always Shop Around for the Best Deal!

One of the Internet's best resources for mortgage information and current rates is Bankrate.com, a free service offered by Bankrate, Inc., the Internet's leading aggregator of financial rate information. The rate data offered by Bankrate.com is obtained by continually surveying approximately 4,800 financial institutions in all 50 states. This allows the service to provide clear, objective, and unbiased rate information. Home buyers and homeowners looking to refinance will find on Bankrate.com free rate information on more than 300 financial products, including mortgages and home equity loans.

In addition to providing the raw financial data needed for intelligent financing or refinancing decisions, the Bankrate.com web site publishes original and objective personal finance articles and offers referrals to connect borrowers with lenders and mortgage brokers nationwide. While Bankrate.com is advertiser-supported, the editorial content and rates offered by the web site are unbiased.

Throughout this book, you've read how important it is to contact multiple lenders or mortgage brokers in order to find the best refinancing deal you qualify for. If you have above-average or excellent credit and you're shopping for a new mortgage, the Bankrate.com web site (www.bankrate.com) can be an extremely helpful, not just for learning about current rates for popular mortgage products available in your area, but also for finding referrals to brokers or lenders offering those highly competitive rates.

If you are looking to refinance, even if your credit score is only average (in the 600s), the Bankrate.com web site offers a variety of online calculators, tools, and informative articles to help you find the best mortgage rates.

No matter how much research you do online, however, it's still your responsibility to discuss your specific situation with two or three reputable and knowledgeable lenders/brokers to find the best deal for your situation.

Often, those all-too-attractive rates and refinancing deals you see or hear advertised are only for "qualified borrowers," which means people with superior credit and good incomes who meet or exceed all of the lender's strict approval guidelines. Everyone else will have to do extra research and shop around to get the best possible mortgage, refinancing, or home equity loan deal.

Greg McBride is a senior financial analyst at Bankrate.com. In this interview, he offers advice on using the free services offered by Bankrate.com to find the best deals for refinancing.

What exactly is Bankrate.com?

Greg McBride: "Bankrate.com is a personal finance web site. We offer award-winning editorial content, online calculators, and a search engine which can be used to find the best rates on a wide range of consumer banking products, including mortgages and home equity loans. We conduct unbiased editorial surveys, which is how we compile our rate data. We are an advertiser-supported service. The information we offer is provided free to the consumer."

What type of information will someone shopping for the best mortgage rates need to provide when visiting Bankrate.com?

Greg McBride: "If we're talking about mortgages, you'll need to select your geographic area, the desired loan amount, and details about the type of mortgage product you're looking for rates on. Everything we present in terms of mortgage data is targeted to consumers with a 700 or greater credit score. We do, however, cater to consumers with a lower credit score who are searching for home equity loans, for example. By providing a small amount of basic information, Bankrate.com will provide an overview of available rates for various mortgage products. We can also provide referrals to lenders or brokers offering those rates in your area. It's then up to you to contact those referrals to gather more information or embark on the application process."

At what point should someone first access Bankrate.com to begin doing research?

Greg McBride: "I recommend someone use Bankrate.com throughout the process of obtaining a mortgage or refinancing. The goal of our service is to empower the consumer to make better financial decisions. We offer articles and information that someone can learn from starting very early in the process. Borrowers can also use our online calculators to determine their financial situation, what they can afford, and then learn about various mortgage products available. When they're ready, they can shop for the best rates or get help finding a broker or lender to work with. At any point along the way, our online tools can help answer common questions. We hope people will use our site to better educate themselves about the whole mortgage process and all of the different mortgage products available. Because we advocate shopping around for the best deals, our search engine is a powerful tool for making this part of the process faster and easier. Rankrate.com is geared for the novice, but it's also suitable for people who are financially savvy."

If someone uses your search engine to find a broker or lender referral, what should he or she do next?

Greg McBride: "I recommend comparison shopping between at least three different lenders. When you first contact a lender, ask questions, compare the mortgage products each offers, and then focus on rates. Make sure you ask plenty of questions about the mortgage products themselves and the associated rates, costs, and fees."

How should someone who is looking to refinance use Bankrate.com?

Greg McBride: "Start off by using our online refinancing calculator (www.bankrate.com/brm/calc_vml/refi/refi.asp) to see if refinancing makes sense based on your situation. This calculator can help you determine, for example, how quickly you'll break even based on the costs associated with refinancing.

"One strategy I always recommend is that someone interested in refinancing should always contact their current lender first. Not only does this lender already have all of your financial information, which can streamline the application-and-approval process, many lenders will work hard to retain your business. After contacting your existing lender, definitely compare rates with a few other brokers or lenders."

What should someone watch out for when shopping around for the best financing deal?

Greg McBride: "When working with lenders or brokers, don't just focus on the interest rate or what the monthly payment will be. You also need to calculate in the fees involved. When comparing lenders offering similar mortgage products, instead of just focusing on the interest rate, focus on the loan's APR, which reflects the total cost of the loan."

Does it matter whether a person meets with a local loan officer in person, as opposed to working primarily by telephone and e-mail?

Greg McBride: "That boils down to personal preference. But, it's always important to comparison shop. If you plan to visit your local bank, for example, also shop around with some of the larger brokers or lenders. It's your job to become an educated consumer, so you know if you're being offered the best deal you qualify for. The mortgage business is highly commoditized."

More Refinancing Advice from a Branch Manager at Countrywide Home Loans

Countrywide Home Loans, Inc. is the largest mortgage bank in the United States. Todd Godfrey is a loan originator and the branch manager of Countrywide Home Loans in Orange Country, California (888 738-2038, todd_godfrey@country wide.com, www.countrywide.com, or www.toddgodfrey.com). He has over 12 years' worth of experience in the mortgage industry and is ranked in the top one percent of mortgage originators nationwide, based on loan volume and statistics published in *Mortgage Originator* magazine. In this interview, Godfrey offers homeowners advice and strategies about refinancing their mortgage.

What advice do you have for someone who is looking to refinance?

Todd Godfrey: "Make sure that when you shop for rates that you also wind up working with a well-known and reputable lender. Contact several lenders or brokers and compare their good-faith estimates. Don't believe any rate quotes until you've see it in writing, along with the associated fees. Also, be sure to provide your loan officer, mortgage consultant, or loan originator (same job description, different title) with your goals and expectations for the refinance, then request that they provide you with at least two different options when tailoring a loan program to meet your needs. Don't be afraid to explore new loan programs or mortgage products, but make sure that you completely understand them."

What pitfalls should someone look out for when looking to refinance?

Todd Godfrey: "Watch out for rates that are too good to be true. Also, watch out for prepayment penalties related to the loan you wind up with. Never refinance using a mortgage product you don't completely understand. Before refinancing, always develop a short-term and long-term finance plan for your home."

What are the most common mistakes people often make when refinancing?

Todd Godfrey: "Some of the most common mistakes I've seen are that a borrower winds up working with a broker or lender that isn't reputable. This can lead to tremendous problems and huge financial consequences. Another problem is that borrowers don't receive a written good-faith estimate from the lender or broker. Or, if and when they receive a good-faith estimate, the borrower doesn't take the time to read it carefully. This document should be used by the borrower to keep the mortgage professional accountable to the rates and fees initially agreed upon."

What money-saving tips or strategies can you offer for someone looking to refinance?

Todd Godfrey: "Always ask about a 'no-cost refinance' option, which means the lender pays all of the fees. The rate for this may be a bit higher, but mortgage interest is tax-deductible, where refinance fees are not. Always consider long-term savings and costs."

What type of research should someone do before attempting to refinance?

Todd Godfrey: "First, put together a list of objectives or goals for the refinance. Then, ask friends and family for a mortgage broker referral."

When is the best time for someone to refinance?

Todd Godfrey: "It all depends on the borrower's needs and objectives."

What options are available to someone who wants to refinance but is currently having financial or credit problems?

Todd Godfrey: "There are sub-prime lenders who have the ability to work with credit-challenged individuals. Some lenders even offer free credit counseling services. For example, Countrywide's House America program has helped many families with less-than-perfect credit."

What are the most common scams associated with refinancing? How can someone avoid them?

Todd Godfrey: "First, watch out for the famous 'bait and switch' when it comes to quoted rates and terms for a loan. Make sure that you ask for and obtain a good-faith estimate from your lender upfront. Compare your initial good-faith estimate with your final good-faith estimate and HUD-1 when you're about to sign your loan documents at the closing. Don't sign anything unless all of the terms and conditions you agreed to are in writing."

What core qualifications should someone have in order to get the best refinance deal?

Todd Godfrey: "First, there's the borrower's credit history and credit score. From a lender or broker's standpoint, a 'perfect' credit score is at or above 730. This score will help you obtain the best rates available. An 'excellent' credit score is at or above 700. This score will allow you to obtain very good rates, but not always the very best rates. The next tier for a credit score is between 660 and 699. This score range may allow you to obtain decent rates, but places you into a higher rate category due to the added risk being taken on by the lender. The final category of 'A' paper tier rates are typically offered to borrowers with a credit score between 620 and 659.

"The next thing lenders look at is the borrower's income. Keep in mind that in general, lenders and brokers offer the best rates on fully documented loans. This means the borrower provides financial documents, such as W-2s, tax returns, pay stubs, and liquid asset statements, including checking, savings, and investment account statements. By providing this documentation, it mitigates the risk for the lender, because they can completely evaluate the borrower's qualifications based on proven and documented facts. Some lenders, such as Countrywide Home Loans, offer 'Document Relief' for borrowers with excellent credit scores, generally 680 or higher. With programs like Countrywide's Fast and Easy loan, the borrower can state their income and assets, without having to dig out financial documents from the closet, basement, junk drawer, garage, or safe. The Fast and Easy loan, which is basically a stated-income/stated-assets loan, can make the borrowing experience very easy."

How long does the refinancing process typically take? How much time is required of the borrower?

Todd Godfrey: "In a normal market, the refinance should generally take two to four weeks. During a 'refi boom,' when the lenders and brokers are very busy, expect the process to take four to eight weeks, depending on the lender. The mortgage professional you work with should spend time upfront with you, usually between 15 minutes and one hour, to define your needs and goals, and then begin the application process."

Need Cash? Check out Your Other Options

Before refinancing your home, if you're in need of cash, investigate other options available to you to see if one of them makes more financial sense for your situation. Talk with your broker or lender about a second mortgage, a home equity loan, or a home equity line of credit. These types of loans also use your property as collateral. More information about these options can be found in the next chapter.

CHAPTER 7

Alternate Cash-Out
Options for Homeowners

WHAT'S IN THIS CHAPTER

- Why use equity in your home for cash, as opposed to other types of loans?

- An overview of second mortgage options

- The pros and cons of a home equity line of credit

- The pros and cons of home equity loans

Mortgages and Refinancing: Get the Best Rates

As you know, a mortgage allows you to borrow a significant amount of money to buy real estate using your home as collateral. Once you build up equity in your home, it's possible to borrow against that equity, again using your home as collateral. If you default on your mortgage, on a home equity loan, or on a home equity line of credit, the bank or lender can initiate a foreclosure, causing you to lose your home.

If you decide to cash out on your home's equity, there are several ways to do this. First, you can refinance your mortgage. The new mortgage would be for a higher amount than you owe on your current mortgage, allowing you to receive the difference in cash. For example, if your home is appraised at $200,000 and you owe $150,000 on your mortgage, you have $50,000 in equity. When you refinance, the principal of your new mortgage could be $175,000, allowing you to receive $25,000 in cash (not taking into account fees, closing costs, taxes, etc.), yet still retain $25,000 of equity in your home.

The benefit to this is that you receive cash at a lower interest rate than if you were to take out an unsecured loan or use your credit cards, for example. Plus, there are tax advantages, because the interest you pay on your mortgage is tax-deductible, while the interest you pay on other types of loans is not.

In the previous chapter, you learned about refinancing, while in Chapter 5, you learned about some of the many mortgage products for financing or refinancing your home. This chapter explores three other popular ways homeowners can tap into the equity in their home in order to receive cash:

- a second mortgage
- a home equity line of credit
- a home equity loan

MORTGAGE **Whether you choose to refinance** your mortgage, apply for a second mortgage, or obtain a home equity line of credit or HELP a home equity loan, you'll need to work with a knowledgeable, reputable, and experienced mortgage broker or lender. See Chapter 3 for advice on choosing a broker or lender.

What distinguishes these types of loans is that the amount you're able to borrow is almost always directly related to your equity in your home. Especially if the real estate market is good and property values have been on the rise, you may discover you possess more equity in your home than you thought.

When you purchased the home, the down payment you made (the amount of the purchase price you didn't finance) established equity right from the start. For example, if you purchased a $200,000 home with a $170,000 mortgage and a $30,000 down payment, immediately after your closing you had $30,000 of equity in your home. If you've been paying off your mortgage month after month and part of each payment has gone toward the loan's principal, that's how much has been building your equity. So, after five years of paying your mortgage (depending on the terms of your mortgage), you may have built up an additional $10,000 to $15,000 or more in equity.

Now, if the appraised value of your home has gone up, that increase is also considered equity. Thus, if you paid $200,000 for the home, but it's now worth $350,000, your equity has increased by $150,000. This is equity you can borrow against and turn into cash that can be used for a wide range of purposes.

There's another significant difference between a mortgage and a home equity loan or a home equity line of credit: on a mortgage the interest on $1 million is tax-deductible, but on a home equity loan or line of credit only the interest on $100,000 is tax-deductible.

Decisions When Choosing a Loan or Line of Credit

Your broker or lender will be able to help you decide whether refinancing your mortgage, taking out a second mortgage, or obtaining a home equity loan or a home equity line of credit best suits your needs, based on your current financial situation, credit score, and objectives.

In order to get reliable advice, however, you'll need to provide your lender or broker with accurate information and a summary of your goals. You'll need to answer the following questions:

- How much money do you need?
- How will you use the money?
- Do you need the money in one lump sum?

- Can you afford an additional monthly payment? If so, how large a payment?
- Do you want a fixed-rate loan or are you comfortable with a variable-rate loan?
- How long will you need the money? Over what period of time do you plan to pay it back?

Once you've reviewed your situation with a lender or broker and pinpointed your needs, shop around for the best rates, just as you would for a traditional mortgage. Then, once you decide what type of loan you want, be prepared for an application-and-approval process that's very similar to applying for a mortgage. There will be plenty of paperwork to complete, plus you'll need to provide financial documentation, such as W2s, tax returns, bank statements, and pay stubs.

MORTGAGE **Just as there are many types** of mortgage products, each

HELP with very different approval guidelines, the same is true for second mortgages, home equity loans, and HELOCs. To qualify for any of these loans, you'll need to meet the approval guidelines of the lender, who will evaluate your income, employment situation, credit history, and credit scores. The lender will also look at how faithful you've been at making the monthly payments on your current mortgage (late payments can hurt your chances) and evaluate your ability to take on the additional debt and make the additional monthly payment(s).

☆ ☆ **WARNING** ☆ ☆

Failure to repay the loans described in this chapter and meet your obligations to the lender can result in foreclosure on your home because it is being used as collateral. If you won't be able to afford the additional monthly payments to repay this debt, don't use it or you could find yourself homeless and in serious financial trouble.

Is a Second Mortgage Right for You?

A second mortgage works just like a first mortgage. There are many types of mortgage products to choose from, depending on your ability to qualify and your purpose(s). On a second mortgage, however, expect to pay a higher interest rate, because the lender takes on a greater risk regardless of your credit score or credit history. Since the second mortgage uses as collateral property that has already been pledged as collateral for the first mortgage, the rights of the lender of the second mortgage are subordinate to the rights of the lender of the first when it comes to getting any proceeds if the home is sold, for example.

The benefit to this type of loan is that the interest you pay is typically tax-deductible. Plus, you'll be repaying the loan over a long period of time, so the monthly payments tend to be affordable, and the interest rate is lower than if you used a credit card or some other unsecured loan, for example. With this type of loan, you must immediately repay the outstanding balance in full if and when you sell your home.

A second mortgage can be at a fixed rate or an adjustable rate. Qualification requirements vary dramatically based on the lender, your financial situation, and the mortgage product. If, after consulting with a financial planner, accountant, mortgage broker, or lender, you determine that a second mortgage can meet your needs, be sure to shop around for the best rates and terms you qualify for.

Words of Wisdom from Mortgage Consultant Mark Giordani

"As an alternative to high-priced loans from credit cards and other non-secured personal loans, some of my clients prefer the advantages of a second mortgage. Typical uses include paying for school tuition, medical bills, or home improvements, such as adding a garage or an additional room. One thing to look out for with second mortgages is the terms of the loan. Some are written to be fully paid off in 10 years, while others are written to be paid off in 30 years. The shorter the term, the higher the monthly payment will be. Generally speaking, second mortgage loans are fixed-rate mortgages and the payments are amortized payments.

"One potential drawback to a second mortgage, especially if they're used for a no-points/no-closing costs refinance transaction, is that the rates may have to be very high to cover all of the costs associated with the lender

---

offering this type of financing. This is especially true with small loan amounts, under $100,000, on second mortgages.

"The procedure for applying for a second mortgage is no different than applying for a first mortgage, other than that the lender will use the anticipated monthly payment for the second mortgage when calculating your eligibility for the financing when considering your income.

"It's important to understand that a second mortgage can take on the form of a home equity loan or home equity line of credit."

The Pros and Cons of Home Equity Loans

A home equity loan is a type of second mortgage. The borrower receives a single lump sum of money once. The loan has a fixed duration and a fixed interest rate. Thus, the monthly payments remain the same until the debt is repaid. This type of loan can be used for a variety of purposes, such as debt consolidation, home improvements, or a big-ticket item. With this type of loan, you must immediately repay the outstanding balance in full if and when you sell your home.

> ### Words of Wisdom from Mortgage Consultant Mark Giordani
>
> "Home equity loans are a great low- or no-cost way of accessing money from the equity in your home. A home equity loan is often a second mortgage behind an existing

first mortgage. However, someone who owns their home outright and does not currently possess a mortgage can still obtain a first-position home equity loan, which is the same as a first mortgage.

"Depending on the rates and terms of your first mortgage, if applicable, it often works out better to refinance your first mortgage for a larger amount than to take out a second mortgage or home equity loan, especially if there are any costs or fees associated with obtaining the loan. Second mortgages and home equity loans tend to carry higher interest rates and are very dependant upon an accurate property appraisal. The amount you can borrow is limited by your home's current market value, not necessarily what you paid for your home."

A Home Equity Line of Credit Provides Cash When You Need It

The best thing about a HELOC is that it gives you a specified loan amount that you can use anytime within a specified draw or withdrawal period (typically five to 15 years). The funds are available only if you choose to use them by writing a check, using a credit card, or making a telephone money transfer.

You can borrow whatever amount you need up to your limit. You can also borrow as many times as you wish within the draw period, although you need to start paying back the loan as soon you begin using the line of credit.

The terms of this type of loan are more like a credit card with an adjustable interest rate and an annual fee. This type of loan can be used for a wide range of purposes.

Here's one example of how you might use this loan. After the line of credit is opened, you're given a limit of $30,000. You then immediately withdraw $10,000 to consolidate your credit card balances and your other debts. You now have to begin repaying that $10,000, but still have $20,000 available. As you pay back the $10,000, your credit line goes back up. This credit line gives you a tremendous amount of flexibility and can save you money if you use it responsibly.

While there are many types of HELOCs and the terms and rates vary greatly, these are typically adjustable-rate loans. The repayment period on a HELOC is typically longer than the draw/withdrawal period. Typically, when repaying this type of loan, the minimum monthly payment covers only the interest, not the principal. You must repay the outstanding balance in full immediately if and when you sell your home.

To have an extra financial cushion when you need it, it's typically a good strategy to apply for a HELOC and get approved while your credit score is high and after you've been approved for your initial mortgage. You never have to use the HELOC, but if you have a financial emergency, the money will be available to you immediately when you need it. It's better to apply for this type of loan before you run into any financial problems or emergencies.

☆ ☆ **WARNING** ☆ ☆

Since this type of loan has an adjustable rate, your required monthly payments could rise, even if your income doesn't. Plus, if the value of your home drops when you decide to sell it, you could wind up earning less on the sale than you owe on the loan.

Words of Wisdom from Mortgage Consultant Mark Giordani

"In terms of qualifying for a HELOC, the process is the same as applying for a mortgage or home equity loan in terms of the time and paperwork involved. The major advantage of a HELOC is that the balance can go up and down, depending on how you want to use it. It's very flexible, like a credit card, but with generally lower rates than a credit card. Another advantage of a HELOC is that the payment is generally calculated as an interest-only payment, so that for the same amount of money borrowed, a home equity line of credit will have a lower monthly payment than a home equity loan, assuming the interest rate is the same.

"A disadvantage of a HELOC is that the interest rate most often is a variable rate that is tied to the prime rate. If the prime rate changes, your monthly payments increase or decrease accordingly. The other disadvantage

---

to a HELOC is that unlike a credit card, the loan taken against your home is secured by your home. Should you be unable to make the monthly payments, the bank/lender may foreclose on your property. This is not generally the case with credit card debt.

"There are some newer HELOC products that do offer fixed rates on the entire balance or some portion thereof. Brokers and lenders sometimes earn their fees based on the amount of money that you actually borrow from the home equity line of credit. If you take out a home equity line for $100,000, do not be surprised if your bank or broker requires you to draw a minimum of approximately $20,000 off the line. In some cases, if you do not draw or use the HELOC, the company that is providing it to you only earns minimal fees and cannot cover the costs of providing a line that goes completely unused. Be sure to discuss draw requirements, annual fees, and early-termination fees with your lender on any home equity line.

"It is also essential to know how your interest rate will adjust if you have an adjustable-rate HELOC. The best time to get a HELOC established on your home is when purchasing your home if you have the equity to qualify. By doing it at that time, you will have access to the line in the event of an emergency. Because you are qualifying for it at the time of getting your first mortgage, it may cost less to obtain and your broker/lender may be able to give you a break on the fees that you would otherwise have to pay. You'll also need to provide your financial documentation only once, so the application process is streamlined."

MORTGAGE ***Prime rate***—This is the interest rate at which commercial financial institutions make short-term loans to borrowers **TERMS** whose credit is so good that there is little risk to the lender. This rate fluctuates based on economic conditions and may differ among financial institutions. The prime rate serves as a basis for the interest rates charged for other loans for which the risk is higher.

☆ ☆ **WARNING** ☆ ☆

Using a HELOC or a home equity loan to consolidate your debt can potentially save you money on your overall monthly payments. However, over the long term you may wind up paying more in interest charges, especially if you take 20 or 30 years to repay the loan. It's important to crunch the numbers and calculate your potential savings in the short term and long term before moving forward with any type of loan.

Always Be Responsible with Your Spending

While a second mortgage, home equity loan, or HELOC can make a large sum of cash available to you, this is money that you ultimately need to pay back—with interest. Spend it responsibly! If you're using the money you receive to consolidate your other debts or to fix some past financial mistakes, learn from those mistakes and don't repeat them in the future.

As a homeowner, it's vital that you develop a monthly budget that allows you to live within your means. It's equally important to stick to that budget. If you need help establishing a budget, seek the guidance of an accountant (CPA) or financial planner. If you've run into problems with credit, work with a reputable credit counselor to remedy the situation. Part of being a responsible homeowner involves learning how to deal with the financial responsibilities of owning and maintaining your home.

The final chapter of this book focuses on the closing process related to a mortgage or refinance.

CHAPTER 8

Alternate Cash-Out
Options for Homeowners

WHAT'S IN THIS CHAPTER

- What to expect at your closing
- What you'll need to bring to your closing
- Closing on a home purchase vs. a refinance
- Avoiding common problems and pitfalls at your closing

Mortgages and Refinancing: Get the Best Rates

The process of buying your home or refinancing your mortgage is almost over! One of the final steps in the process is the *closing* (aka *settlement*). This is when all of the contracts and legal documents get signed and, if the closing is on a home, the property changes ownership from the seller to the buyer. Don't worry! Your real estate attorney, your real estate agent (if you're buying a home), and potentially your mortgage broker will be present during this process to guide you. Be prepared to sign dozens upon dozens of legal documents, forms, and contracts.

At the closing, all of the parties may be present—you and the people listed above and, if you're buying a home, the seller and his or her attorney and real estate agent. The closing agent (or an attorney) will conduct the meeting. It's that person's job to collect all of the necessary paperwork in advance and make sure that all documents are ready to be signed. When all of the parties attend the closing, it's called a *round table closing*. However, a closing can also take place with each party separately, using an escrow process overseen by the closing agent. This is called an *escrow closing*.

You may hear the terms *wet settlement* and *dry settlement*. A *wet settlement* is when the funds are available for the closing and the seller gets them right away. The closing agent is there with a cashier's check or the money is wired into the seller's account at the same time as the parties are closing. A *dry settlement* is when there is no money for the seller at the closing. Usually, the settlement company or attorney will complete the documents and submit them to the lender for review; then the lender will provide the funds.

MORTGAGE
HELP

When refinancing, the closing will typically take place either in an attorney's office or in the closing agent's office. The attorney or closing agent will be hired by the mortgage broker or lender. You have the option of having your own attorney present. At this meeting, the paperwork is signed for the new mortgage. (The new loan won't be disbursed, however, until after the rescission period ends if you are refinancing a primary residence.) For additional information about refinancing, obtaining a home equity loan, or taking out a second mortgage, see Chapter 7.

What Is a Closing?

The closing is one of the final steps in the home-buying or refinancing process. It takes place when the buyer and the seller have reached an agreement, the necessary financing has been approved, and all of the documents necessary for the transaction have been prepared and are ready to be signed. Prior to the closing, you must obtain a *letter of commitment* from your lender, stating that you have been approved for the mortgage and that the funds will be made available to you at the closing.

MORTGAGE
TERMS

Letter of commitment—A letter from the mortgage broker or lender stating that you've been approved for a mortgage and specifying the amount of the loan and the terms.

At the closing, if you're buying a home, the terms of the

agreement between you and the seller will be reviewed. At the same time, the terms of the agreement between you and your mortgage lender will also be reviewed. When all of the documents have been signed, you will receive your mortgage (the money you're borrowing). If you're buying a home, you and the seller will execute the sales contract; at this point, ownership of the home transfers from the seller to you. Finally, all of the various fees and expenses associated with the purchase or refinancing are distributed to the appropriate parties.

The scheduling of your closing can be a tricky process, because it must happen before the *loan commitment* you receive from your lender expires, but you need ample time to ensure that all of the necessary paperwork is completed and that, if you're buying a home, any work on the home has been finished prior to the closing. If you're buying a home, your real estate agent or the seller's agent will provide guidance and probably schedule the closing at the appropriate time. If you're refinancing, the mortgage broker or lender will schedule the closing.

If you're buying a home, within 24 hours before the closing, make an appointment to walk through the home and conduct a final inspection. Depending on the situation, your real estate agent should be present. You might also want to bring along a home inspector, if any construction or major repair work has recently been done on the home. The purpose of this walk-through is to ensure that there's been no recent damage to the home and that the seller has completed all of the repairs to which he or she has agreed. At this point, the home should be in the condition specified in your purchase and sale agreement.

During the final inspection, make sure that everything is present that was specified in the purchase and sale agreement as included with the house. This might include appliances, window treatments, lighting fixtures, and furniture. If you haven't negotiated for these items to be included in the purchase and they're not listed in the purchase and sale agreement, you're not entitled to them.

MORTGAGE HELP **Some states require the buyer/homeowner** to have an attorney representing him or her at the closing. Regardless of what your state requires, hiring a competent real estate attorney to be with you at the closing and to review all of the documents before you sign them is an excellent strategy to ensure that all of your legal and financial interests are being met. For a refi, an attorney does not typically need to be present, but you should still review all of the paperwork in advance and not rely on the closing agent or the lender's attorney to look out for your best interests.

You have the right to request copies of all paperwork 24 hours in advance of the closing, so you and your attorney have ample time to review them. This is an opportunity to ensure that everything you've agreed to is stated properly in the documents that will become legally binding as soon as you sign them at the closing.

Be Prepared at the Closing

At the closing, you'll need to sign dozens of legal documents. It's the closing agent's responsibility to prepare all of the documents in advance. However, mistakes and typos happen, so it's a good idea to review everything.

You are responsible for providing the following at or before the closing:

- If you're closing on a home, a copy of your new homeowner's insurance policy and copies of all related insurance policies, plus proof of payment for those policies, so you can show they're in force.

- If you're closing on a home, a certified check to cover all closing costs and your down payment on the home. The closing agent will tell you the exact amount of that check prior to the closing. Personal checks are rarely accepted. If you plan to wire the funds, coordinate this transaction several days in advance. Of course, cash is always accepted.

- One or two forms of photo identification (driver's license and/or passport) to prove your identity prior to signing any documents.

- If you're refinancing, a certified check to cover any out-of-pocket expenses. In many cases, the fees associated with refinancing can be built into the loan, which means that at the closing you will have no out-of-pocket expenses.

MORTGAGE **The money due at the closing** will be specified on the HUD-1
Settlement Statement, which the closing agent should provide
HELP to you at least 24 hours prior to the closing. The HUD-1 lists
all of the services provided and the associated fees that you are
responsible for paying. You should be aware of and approve all of
these fees in advance. You can see the HUD-1 Settlement
Statement here: www.hudclips.org/sub_nonhud/html/pdfforms/
1.pdf.

Fees Associated with the Closing

Buying a home isn't cheap. Many people receive fees in order
for this process to happen. If you're buying a home, here are
some of the fees you'll be responsible to pay at the closing:

- **Appraisal fee**—This, typically under $350 for a single-
family home or condominium, is to be paid when the
appraisal is done or before the work is done. The
appraisal helps to determine the current value of the
home you're buying or refinancing and is required by
the lending (mortgage) company. The appraisal is con-
ducted by an independent, licensed professional. Your
lender will typically choose the appraiser, although you
will be responsible for the fee.

- **Application fee**—Depending on the situation, you may
be required to pay the application fee for the mortgage
when you apply for it. This fee is intended to cover
what it costs the lender or mortgage broker to process
your application. This fee varies dramatically from

company to company and what you pay could, in part, be determined by your credit score and the type of mortgage.

- **Loan origination fee**—The lender or mortgage broker charges this fee to offset the institution's costs and earn a profit. This fee can be a percentage of the loan amount. Loan origination fees vary greatly, so it's important to shop around for the best deals and negotiate.

- **Discount points**—You pay this fee at the closing to lower the interest rate on your loan. Basically, it allows you to prepay finance charges in order to save money over the life of the loan.

- **Taxes**—These are fees charged by local governments to transfer ownership of the property. The taxes collected at the closing could also represent prorated annual real estate (property) taxes that are due. The taxes will vary greatly, depending on where the home is located. These fees cannot be negotiated down. However, you may be able to split them with the seller, if you negotiate this in advance.

- **Miscellaneous fees**—Depending on your situation, you may be required to pay other fees at the closing, which will be outlined in advance. For example, if you're taking over the seller's mortgage, you may be required to pay a transfer or assumption fee. If you're purchasing a condominium, you may be required to pay condominium fees at the closing.

MORTGAGE

TERMS

*Closing costs—*These are all fees, charges, and taxes you'll be required to pay at the closing. Each fee, charge, and tax will be itemized on the HUD-1 statement and can include payment required for points, taxes, title insurance, and financing costs.

Some of the other charges for which you may be responsible (which will be listed on the HUD-1) are administrative fees, credit report retrieval fees, underwriting fees, title examination fees, title insurance fees, document preparation fees, escrow fees, pest inspection fees, recording fees, and survey fees. If you're buying a home and not refinancing, you may also have to pay fees to your real estate agent. Depending on the situation, it's not uncommon for fees due at closing to be $10,000 or more. It is sometimes possible, however, to build some or all of these fees into the loan, so you pay little or nothing out of pocket at the closing. Fees for a refi are often lower, depending on the situation.

MORTGAGE

HELP

Some out the fees can be negotiated in advance so you can potentially save money. Certain fees have fixed rates and cannot be adjusted or waived.

Navigating Through Piles and Piles of Paperwork

Despite the fact that computers play a key role in just about everything, when it comes to the closing, virtually all of paperwork is done traditionally, using paper. Consequently, hundreds of sheets of paper are generated in the sale of a home or a refinance.

Some of the documents associated with a closing are the *HUD-1 Settlement Statement*, the *truth-in-lending statement*, the *mortgage note*, and the *deed of trust*. Your attorney will review each of these documents with you. Take the time to ensure that all of the numbers, terms, and information on these forms and contracts are accurate before signing them. Regardless of any verbal agreements you reach with the seller (if you're buying a home) or the lender, it's whatever is in black and white within these documents that will be legally binding.

☆ ☆ **WARNING** ☆ ☆

A dishonest mortgage broker or lender may make last-minute changes in the loan terms, such as raising the interest rate. You may never have discussed these changes, but they could appear in the paperwork at the closing. If you sign documents with changes, you are legally accepting these changes because the documents are then legally binding. By working with an attorney who represents you (not the seller or the lender), you reduce the chances of this happening.

Mortgage note—This is the formal written agreement between the home buyer and the lender. It's a legally binding agreement that includes the buyer's promise to repay the debt. It also details the terms of the loan and specifies penalties that could be imposed if payments are late or missed or if the loan goes into default.

MORTGAGE
TERMS

MORTGAGE ***Deed of trust**—*If the home buyer fails to meet his or her financial obligations and make monthly mortgage payments, TERMS this document gives the lender legal claim to the home and property. It also includes a summary of the legal rights of both the lender and the borrower, such as the ability of the lender to foreclose on the home if the loan goes into default.

If you're buying a home, here are some of the many other documents you may be required to sign at the closing:

- *Name affidavit*—a document listing your full name and all of the aliases you currently use or have used in the past
- *Occupancy affidavit*—a document stating that you intend to live in the home you're purchasing and that it will be your primary residence
- *Payment letter*—a document that specifies your monthly mortgage payment, when it's due, and where you should send it
- *Form 4506*—an IRS form, *Request for Copy of Tax Form*, allowing the lender to obtain and review copies of your tax returns and other tax-related documents to verify your income

Shortly after your closing (or perhaps several months later), your loan may be transferred to another lender or investor that will then service it (i.e., collect your monthly mortgage payments). This is a common practice. At the closing you will be notified if this is a possibility.

Mortgages and Refinancing: Get the Best Rates

Depending on the type of mortgage, your monthly payment will most likely consist of four components—principal, interest, taxes, and insurance. If the down payment on your home is less than 20 percent of the purchase price, you'll most likely need to acquire *private mortgage insurance (PMI)*, which you will pay in advance at the closing or will be added into your monthly mortgage payments. If you have a good credit score, there are several strategies for avoiding the necessity of paying PMI; your broker can advise you.

Although you'll be confronted at the closing with hundreds of papers to review and sign, there's no need to become anxious, especially if you have a real estate attorney sitting next to you reviewing all of the documents and explaining their significance before you sign them. Assuming that all of the parties show up for the closing on time and all of the paperwork is in order, the closing should take under one hour.

Unfortunately, it's common for mistakes to be noticed in the paperwork or for documents to be missing at the closing. Don't panic if this happens. Your attorney will know exactly how to proceed and advise you accordingly. Typically, unless a mistake is significant, the closing will continue on schedule and small corrections to documents will be made later. In some situations, it may be necessary to delay the closing until all of the documents are corrected and ready to be signed.

Closing-Related Mistakes to Avoid

In the days and weeks leading up to your closing, there are some things you should do to avoid unnecessary complications.

For example, refrain from making any major purchases or applying for credit cards. Purchasing a car or other big-ticket item could cause problems with the mortgage broker or lender. If you need to make a major purchase, wait until after the closing to ensure that it won't affect your credit score or somehow jeopardize your ability to get approved for the mortgage.

Also, in the weeks leading up to your closing, don't change jobs. Obviously, this includes not getting laid off or fired. This could negatively impact the approval process for your mortgage. Lenders typically prefer a consistent job history. If you need to change employers, do this after the closing. (Earning a raise or promotion with your current employer is fine.)

The following paragraphs apply if you're buying a home, not refinancing.

If you'll be paying money to the seller, such as the down payment, make sure this money goes into a trust or escrow account until the closing. You don't want the seller spending your money before the house is officially yours.

In addition to homeowner's insurance and mortgage insurance, consider hazard insurance and make sure your new home is insured adequately. To avoid any complications at the closing, make sure you acquire all of the necessary insurance in advance and that you have the paperwork to prove that you've paid for the policies and they're in force.

Make sure you schedule a final walk-through of the home the day before the closing. Your real estate agent will help you tie up any loose ends and make sure everything is ready for the closing. During your walk-through, if you notice any problems, make sure you bring them to the attention of the seller and your real estate agent immediately. For example, as the seller was moving out of the home, perhaps damage to a doorway or wall happened. You want to ensure that the seller will take care of repairing the damage prior to the closing. This walk-through should be in addition to a professional inspection, which should be completed by an independent home inspector who will be able to explore the home and identify problems and defects that you might not notice.

During the home inspection, the inspector will check for potential problems with the following, in particular:

- Air conditioning and heating system
- Basement and foundation
- Electrical system and wiring
- Interior and exterior framing and overall construction
- Plumbing
- Roof
- Ventilation and insulation

MORTGAGE

HELP

Just prior to the closing, your lender will supply you with a list of documents you'll need to bring with you to the closing. To avoid delays, remember to bring everything that's expected.

☆ ☆ **WARNING** ☆ ☆

The listing agent or the real estate agent who represents the seller does not represent you, the buyer! This person will *not* be working in your best interest, financially or otherwise. No matter how professional and pleasant the agent is to you, never assume he or she is offering you the best price or giving you all of the information you need to make a well-informed purchase decision. This is also true of real estate attorneys representing the seller or lender. Unless you hired the attorney to represent you, he or she can not provide you with legal advice and is in no way obligated to look out for your best interests.

Another common mistake among home buyers is making verbal agreements with the seller and/or the lender. Everything you agree to should ultimately be documented in writing and then both parties should sign and date the documents. This ensures a mutual and legally binding understanding of the agreement.

Perhaps the biggest mistake home buyers make is taking on too much debt. Before the closing, review all of the numbers and your budget. Make sure you can afford to purchase the home and will be able to stay current on your mortgage payments, properly maintain the home, and be able to afford all of the costs associated with owning a home, such as insurance and real estate taxes. Hopefully, you've done all of your financial calculations and budgeting much earlier in the process. Just because you've been approved for a large mortgage to cover the cost of the home doesn't necessarily mean you can afford it. It's up to you to make this determination—not the lender or mortgage broker.

If you're refinancing, make sure the refi will actually allow you to achieve your financial objectives and the new loan makes financial sense for you. Don't rely on promises by the lender or broker. Crunch the numbers for yourself and determine if you'll be saving money and what your break-even point will be. If the refi is not allowing you to achieve your objectives but it's costing you money in fees and closing costs, walk away from the deal.

Depending on the type of mortgage you're acquiring, make sure that if for some reason real estate prices in your area drop, but you haven't built up a lot of equity in your new home, you won't wind up owing more money than the home is worth. You could always hang onto the home in hopes real estate values will rise again, but if you need to sell at some point in order to relocate for a job, you could run into costly problems if you're overextended financially.

The Closing Experts Speak Out

Based in Roswell, Georgia, Homestead Settlement Solutions (678 277-9660, www.homesteadsettlements.com) is a one-stop shop that handles real estate closings nationwide. The company was founded in 2004 by two former National Football League players, Adam Walker and Sean Vanhorse.

Between 1992 and 1996, Walker was a running back for the San Francisco 49ers and then the Philadelphia Eagles. He was a four-time member of NFC West Championship Teams and a member of the 1994 San Francisco 49ers Super Bowl XXIX Championship Team.

Between 1990 and 1997, Vanhorse was a defensive cornerback for the Miami Dolphins, the San Diego Chargers, the Detroit Lions, and the Minnesota Vikings. In 1994, he was a member of the AFC Championship Team and a member of the 1994 San Diego Chargers Super Bowl XXIX Team.

Since leaving the NFL, the two athletes have built up a company that's dedicated to providing quality services to clients seeking assistance with closings, title services, appraisals, and valuation services. In this interview, Walker and Vanhorse offer advice for ensuring that your closing goes smoothly and you avoid unnecessary costs or delays.

How did you go from being a professional football player in the NFL to founding Homestead Settlement Solutions?

Adam Walker: "I am a graduate of the University in Pittsburgh with a degree in economics. Through the years,

I have worked for a variety of different financial and real estate companies. My partners and I saw a need for a one-stop shop to handle closing services and we pooled our collective knowledge and professional backgrounds, which included real estate development and real estate law, to form Homestead Settlement Solutions."

Can a borrower decide what company will be hired to handle his or her closing?

Adam Walker: "This depends on the state you're in. In some cases, the lender chooses the company that will handle the closing. For those states that require an attorney to be present at the closing, we have developed a nationwide network of lawyers. The borrower often has an option to choose what company will handle their closing, especially for home purchases. For refinances and home equity loans, the lender typically chooses the closing company. The fact that the borrower often has a right to choose their closing company isn't something lenders typically disclose. By hiring your choice of companies to handle your closing, you could potentially save money. When looking for a company to handle a closing, you want to find an organization that's fast, efficient, experienced, and affordable."

If a closing goes without a hitch, how long should it take?

Adam Walker: "A typical closing lasts about one hour. However, if any problems are uncovered with the paperwork, for example, this can cause delays. I recommend allowing at least two hours. This is rarely something you can do during your lunch hour."

Regardless of what the local law stipulates, should a home buyer or borrower have an attorney represent him or her and attend the closing?

Adam Walker: "This is a personal decision. Many people choose to save the expense of hiring their own attorney, which typically involves paying their hourly fee, plus travel time to and from the closing. Having an attorney represent you provides you with peace of mind. The attorney or closing agent that is present but not hired by you always represents the lender, not the buyer or the seller. One thing an attorney can help prevent is the borrower paying for the same services twice because they're worded differently on the HUD-1 statement."

What is the main difference between a closing for a home purchase and a refinance?

Adam Walker: "The actual paperwork that needs to be signed is almost always very similar. The big difference is that with a refinance, there's a three-day rescission period. This gives the borrower three days to decide to negate the new mortgage simply by notifying the lender or closing agent."

When reviewing the paperwork before signing it at the closing, what should the borrower look for?

Adam Walker: "Make sure all of the rates and fees quoted are the same. Bring the good-faith estimate and HUD-1 statement you were given prior to the closing and make sure all of the numbers in the final paperwork match up and that no changes have been made. Often, borrowers expect that the closing process will go smoothly. However, problems do often arise that need to be dealt with. If changes or corrections need to be made to the paperwork on the spot, this can delay the proceedings.

"One cause of potential delays is that people don't realize personal checks are typically not accepted for any fees that are due at the closing. If you need to bring money to the closing to pay certain fees, arrange in advance for a certified bank check, have cash on hand, or determine how that money will be paid.

"If the borrower doesn't have anyone representing them at the closing and their broker or Realtor® isn't present, the first thing the borrower should do when a problem arises is pick up the phone and call their broker, lender, and/or Realtor®. The goal is to make sure the loan closes by overcoming the problems on the spot."

What are some of the most common problems a borrower might experience at the closing?

Adam Walker: "The most common problem we see is that the borrower didn't fully understand the mortgage product they were getting until everything was laid out at the closing. Many people opt to back out of the loan at the closing because they weren't fully informed of the ramifications pertaining to the adjustable-rate loan or interest-only loan, for example, they've qualified for. In some cases, the borrower wasn't informed in advance about certain costs or fees, such as taxes or insurance. Upon doing the last-minute calculations, the borrower realizes he or she can't afford the loan."

What can a borrower do in advance to ensure that the closing goes smoothly?

Sean Vanhorse: "Carefully review all of the paperwork beforehand and understand what fees you'll be expected to pay at the closing. You'll also need to bring proper identification to the closing."

At the closing, is it too late to start negotiating fees associated with closing costs?

Sean Vanhorse: "Yes. As soon as you receive a truth-in-lending statement, a good-faith estimate, and later your HUD-1 prior to the closing, review all of the fees and costs and do your negotiating then. The only reason why you'd want to negotiate at the closing is if unexpected fees are being charged to you. The borrower always has the power prior to the closing and during the closing to walk away. Disagreements about fees can often be resolved at the closing, especially if the borrower has their own attorney representing them. Ordinarily, the closing is not the time to be negotiating fees. This can cause delays in the closing process.

"Prior to the closing, ask to be informed of any changes to the HUD-1 or the contracts. Any changes can impact fees and costs. Try to handle any disputes before the closing."

What is title insurance? Is it necessary?

Sean Vanhorse: "Title insurance is an insurance policy that protects the homebuyer against there being any liens or judgments against the property after they've taken ownership of it. The cost of title insurance is based on the value of the home. Many lenders require the borrower to acquire title insurance. If you do not have this insurance, as the homebuyer, you are responsible for any problems with the title that happen down the road. Title insurance can be acquired at the closing. In many cases, the cost of this insurance is automatically added to the HUD-1 statement, whether or not it is requested by the homebuyer."

Attorney Laura Egerman Offers Additional Advice on Real Estate Closings

Laura Egerman is a title attorney employed by Equity National Title Insurance Company (800 237-8489, www.equityin.com) in East Providence, Rhode Island. Her responsibilities include reviewing the title work her company receives from title examiners. This involves verifying that the person who has applied for a new mortgage has a legal interest in the property he or she is attempting to mortgage and verifying that the borrower owns the property he or she wants to mortgage.

The title searches she performs reveal the names of the owners of the property and a description of the parcel in question. It shows the mortgages that encumber the property and any other encumbrances, such as judgments or tax liens. While the client service coordinator is responsible for obtaining tax information and mortgage payoff information, Egerman is responsible for obtaining payoffs for judgments. When appropriate, she is also responsible for clearing titles—a process that involves obtaining discharges or satisfactions for mortgages and judgments that have not been satisfied in the land records, though they have been paid.

In time for the closing, Egerman must make certain that the title to the property is clear and that the lien position of her client is not clouded. As a result of her work, she is extremely knowledgeable about the closing process and has participated in hundreds of them. In this interview, Egerman offers additional advice to borrowers about the closing process.

Who attends a closing?

Laura Egerman: "For a purchase, the buyer(s) and the seller(s), their respective Realtors®, and the closing agent. The closing agent can be either an attorney or a notary public, depending on the state. For a refi, the borrower(s) and the closing agent are the only parties that need to attend."

Who is responsible for scheduling the closing, creating the paperwork, and inviting all of the participants?

Laura Egerman: "I can only speak about what happens at my company in this instance. At Equity, the CSC [client service coordinator] is responsible for scheduling the closing at a time convenient for the borrower(s) and the closing agent. We have a network of closing agents in all of the states that we cover and have a list of agents readily available. The paperwork is created by both the lender and by Equity. The lender will send over the closing package, which includes the note, the mortgage and any riders, the truth-in-lending statement, tax documents, and other loan documents, while the CSC prepares the HUD and certain other documents that are unique to our company."

How are a closing for a home and a closing for refinancing different?

Laura Egerman: "The primary difference is when funds are disbursed. When you purchase a home, both the buyer(s) and the seller(s) attend. After all of the documents are signed by both sides, the buyer(s) will receive the keys to the property, while the seller will receive a check for the proceeds of the sale. This amount is the sale price, less deductions to pay off mortgages, Realtors'® commissions, etc. By contrast, after the closing of a refi, the refinancing borrowers get nothing. After the three-day rescission period expires, the loan will disburse and the borrower will receive the proceeds of the transaction, if any, after prior mortgages are repaid and other obligations, such as credit cards, etc., are paid."

How should a borrower prepare for his or her closing?

Laura Egerman: "From my experience, the best thing that a borrower can do is be prepared. Give your loan officer all of the information about your current loans or judgments. All of this information will be revealed in the course of the title search anyway, but the sooner your loan officer is aware of them, the sooner they can start working to obtain payoffs or get releases, so that the closing can proceed on schedule. Also, a loan officer should have reviewed the loan program and the preliminary HUD with the borrowers prior to closing."

Do you recommend that a borrower have an attorney who represents him or her at the closing? When is this appropriate?

Laura Egerman: "Typically, refi borrowers do not have attorneys present. As for purchases, the ones we deal with don't involve attorneys—title companies are used in place of attorneys."

What fees or out-of-pocket expenses will a borrower be paying at the closing?

Laura Egerman: "At a refinance closing, the borrower's out-of-pocket expenses are usually paid outside of the closing and will be listed on the HUD-1 as 'POC' [paid outside of closing]. These items can include application fees, tax service fees, credit report fees, loan origination fees or discount fees, flood certifications, etc. In certain instances a refinance may be a 'cash in' deal, where the borrowers will have to pay some money at closing in order to obtain a certain interest rate or qualify for a specific loan program. The majority of fees are simply deducted from the proceeds of the closing.

"At a purchase closing, the fees are similar to those for the refinance, but can also include Realtor® commissions, etc. All of the possible fees are listed on the second page of the HUD." [To see a sample HUD-1 statement, visit www.hud.gov/ offices/hsg/sfh/res/sc3sectd.cfm.]

What are some of the most common problems a borrower can expect during the closing? How can they be avoided?

Laura Egerman: "With refinances, the most common issues we see come up at the table are related to the mortgage. The borrower is unhappy with the terms of the mortgage, such as the interest rate, a prepayment penalty, or another technical issue. These issues often relate directly to the amount of money that the borrower will receive as proceeds from the closing. A good loan officer will have explained the loan program to the borrower in sufficient detail prior to the closing, so there are no surprises."

What can a borrower do to avoid delays at the closing?

Laura Egerman: "Have all of your documents in order and be sure to communicate all possible issues to your loan officer prior to the closing."

What happens immediately after the closing?

Laura Egerman: "After a purchase closing, the buyer(s) get the keys to their new home. The executed mortgage or deed of trust, depending on the state, is taken to the local registry for recording in the land records. The money from closing is used to pay off the seller's mortgage(s), if any, or other liens against the property and other charges incurred by or on behalf of the seller to consummate the closing. The seller receives a check for the proceeds of the sale, which is the sale price, less all payoffs made on seller's behalf and other charges incurred by seller.

"After a refinance closing, after the rescission period expires, the loan is disbursed, with mortgages and/or other debts being paid off. The proceeds are sent to the borrower. The mortgage is also sent for recording in the local land records."

Do you have any tips for understanding the HUD-1 statement and/or the truth-in-lending statement?

Laura Egerman: "The HUD-1 is simple to understand. The first page is the 'summary sheet.' On the left side of the page is the summary of the borrower's transaction, such as the amounts to be paid by the borrower in order to consummate the purchase or refinance. On the right side of the page is the summary of the seller's transaction, such as the amounts to be paid by the seller and amounts to be received by the seller.

"Page two of the HUD shows, in detail, the charges being

paid at closing and by whom they are being paid. Often, in a refinance transaction, the borrower will be paying off credit card obligations or cars or other debts. If the list of items being paid is long, an addendum will be attached to the HUD listing each item to be paid."

What is a cooling-off period? When and how does it apply? How long does it last?

Laura Egerman: "At the closing for a refinance, the borrower will receive the Notice of Right to Cancel statement, as required by law. The borrower has three business days from whenever the events enumerated on the notice occurred to cancel the transaction, for whatever reason.

"If the borrower wishes to cancel the transaction, it must be done in writing by signing the Notice of Right to Cancel form and submitting it to the lender. The lender thereafter has 20 calendar days to take the steps necessary to show that there is no lien against your property in favor of the lender. Keep in mind, there is no effect on liens remaining in existence at the time you cancel. At this time, the lender must also return to the borrower any funds collected for the transaction. The borrower, however, does not need to return any funds extended to him by the lender, until the lender has complied with the requirements for terminating its lien against the property."

What is title insurance? Why is it needed? What does it protect? Do you have any advice for buying it?

Laura Egerman: "It's important to understand there are two types of coverage, which include lender's policies and owner's policies. An owner's policy is usually purchased in connection with a purchase. The policy ensures that the buyer takes clear title to the property and that there is nothing that precludes his total lawful ownership of the property. Similarly, a lender's policy ensures that the lender's interest in the property, which is conveyed via the mortgage, is free and clear.

"Most lenders require a lender's policy for loans. The cost is paid by the borrower. Owner's policies are not required. Whether to purchase one is completely up to the buyer."

Congratulations—the Process Is Complete!

If you were buying a home, you're now officially a homeowner! The deed for the property and the house keys will be in your hands. You are now responsible for making your monthly mortgage payments on time for the term of the mortgage. If you were refinancing your home, your new mortgage will go into effect immediately after the three-day rescission period ends.

Once the closing has ended, you'll be given copies of the documents you've signed. Keep all of these papers together in a safe place. You'll need to refer back to them in the future if and when you decide to refinance your mortgage or sell the home.

Hopefully, this book has provided you with the core

knowledge you need to be an educated borrower, whether obtaining a mortgage or refinancing your home. Reading this book is only the first step, however. It's important to ask plenty of questions when working with a lender or broker, plus do your own research in the vast resources on the Web. Obtaining a mortgage or refinancing your home can be a time-consuming and confusing process. By doing your homework, however, you can ensure that the process goes smoothly and doesn't wind up costing you extra.

For help dealing with other personal finance issues, be sure to read some of the other books in the growing library of *Entrepreneur Personal Finance Pocket Guides*. You can learn more about available titles at www.entrepreneurpress.com or www.jasonrich.com.

Web Site Directory

The following is a list of the web sites and online resources mentioned in this book.

A-Loan-Calculator.com—www.a-loan-calculator.com

AnnualCreditReport.com—www.annualcreditreport.com

Bank of America loan calculators—www.bankofamerica.com/loansandhomes/index.cfm

Bankrate.com—www.bankrate.com

Bankrate.com refinancing calculator—www.bankrate.com/ brm/calc_vml/refi/refi.asp

Bankrate.com moving calculator—www.bankrate.com/ brm/movecalc.asp

Better Business Bureau—www.bbb.org

CityRating.com cost of living calculator—www.cityrating. com/costofliving.asp

CNN cost of living calculator—cgi.money.cnn.com/tools/ costofliving/costofliving.html

Countrywide Home Loans—www.countrywide.com or www.toddgodfrey.com

Equifax—www.equifax.com

Equity National Title Insurance Company—www.equityin. com

Experian—www.experian.com

FHA—www.hud.gov

FICO® Score—www.MyFICO.com

HomeGain.com mortgage comparison—www.homegain.com

Homestead Settlement Solutions—www.homesteadsettle-ments.com

Just Mortgage Calculators—www.justmortgagecalculators. com

LendingTree.com—www.lendingtree.com

LowerMyBills.com—www.lowermybills.com

Monster Board Salary Wizard—promotions.monster.com/ salary

Mortgage101.com—www.mortgage101.com

Mortgage101.com loan calculators—www.mortgage101.com

Mortgage Bankers Association—www.mortgagebankers.org

Move, Inc. mortgage payment calculator—finance.realtor.com/HomeFinance/calculators/mortgage-payment.asp

MyFICO.com FICO Score online—www.myfico.com

National Association of Realtors—www.realtor.com or www.realtor.org

Sperling's Best Places—www.bestplaces.net/col

TransUnion—www.transunion.com

U.S. Department of Housing and Urban Development (HUD) HUD-1 Settlement Statement sample—www.hud-clips.org/sub_nonhud/html/pdfforms/1.pdf or www.hud.gov/offices/hsg/sfh/res/sc3sectd.cfm

U.S. Department of Housing and Urban Development (HUD) real estate glossary—www.hud.gov/offices/ hsg/sfh/buying/glossary.cfm

U.S. Department of Housing and Urban Development (HUD) workshops—www.hud.gov/buying /localbuying.cfm

U.S. Department of Veterans Affairs—www.homeloans. va.gov

WakefieldSoft, LLC—www.wakefieldsoft.com

Wikipedia mortgage broker—en.wikipedia.org/wiki/ Mortgage_broker

Yahoo! Finance loan calculators—Finance.yahoo.com/ loan/mortgage

Yahoo! Real Estate—realestate.yahoo.com/re/neighbor-hood/mail.html

Yahoo! Real Estate amortization calculator—realestate. yahoo.com/calculators/amortization.html

Yahoo! Real Estate glossary—realestate.yahoo.com/loans/ glossary.html

Glossary

The following is a glossary of important mortgage, credit, and finance terms used throughout this book. Understanding these terms will help you to better find and negotiate your best mortgage or refinancing deal.

Adjustable-rate mortgage (ARM)—A loan with an interest rate that can change during the life of the loan. If the interest rate goes down, so does the monthly payment (in most cases). If the interest rate goes up, so does the monthly payment. There are several types of ARMs. Some mortgages start off with a fixed interest rate and convert to an adjustable rate after a specified period. The amount the interest rate can change is often subject to a cap.

Amortization—The repayment of a loan, such as a mortgage, in which part of the payment is applied to the principal balance.

AnnualCreditReport.com—A centralized service operated by the three credit reporting agencies (credit bureaus) that processes all requests from consumers who wish to receive their free credit report from each agency.

Annual percentage rate (APR)—The yearly rate of interest that includes all fees and costs paid to acquire the loan (such as interest, mortgage insurance, certain closing costs, and points paid at closing). All lenders are obligated by law to disclose a loan's APR.

Appraisal—An estimate of a property's fair market value calculated by a professional, licensed appraiser.

Broker associate—The person who works for the mortgage broker who is a borrower's primary contact throughout the application, approval, and closing process. Also known as a *mortgage consultant* or a *loan officer*, this person will often work on a commission basis, based on the mortgage products he or she sells.

Cash-out—The process of refinancing and borrowing more money than is owed on a mortgage in order to obtain cash.

Closing—The formal sale of a property and transfer from seller to buyer, when the buyer also formally acquires the mortgage and pays all closing costs and the seller provides the title for the property.

Closing costs—All fees, charges, and taxes the buyer will be required to pay at the closing, (possibly including payment for points), taxes, title insurance, and financing costs.

Conforming loan—Any type of mortgage that meets the criteria and limits set forth by the largest buyers of loans, including *Fannie Mae* or *Freddie Mac*.

Correspondent lender—A hybrid company that offers borrowers the benefits of working with a direct lender and the flexibility of working with a broker who represents many mortgage products, typically at more competitive rates than ordinary brokers. A correspondent lender makes approval decisions and initially funds the loan, but then, upon closing the loan, the correspondent lender sells the loan to another lender for servicing.

Credit rating—An educated estimate of a person's creditworthiness, a prediction of the likelihood that the person will pay a debt and the extent to which the lender is protected in the event of default.

Credit report—A credit file disclosure compiled by one of the credit reporting agencies—Equifax, Experian, or TransUnion—that contains personal and financial information about a person, including name, address, phone number, Social Security number, date of birth, past addresses, current and past employers, a listing of companies that have issued credit to that person (including credit cards, charge cards, car loans, mortgages, student loans, and home equity loans), and details about his or her credit history.

Credit reporting agency (aka credit bureau)—Any of the three national bureaus—Equifax, Experian, and TransUnion—that maintain credit histories on virtually all Americans with any credit history and supply creditors and lenders with timely and reliable financial reports as requested.

Credit score—A mathematical calculation of a person's creditworthiness, in which a credit reporting agency applies a complex formula to his or her current financial situation and credit history. A credit score will be between 300 and 850. The national average is about 678. To qualify for a mortgage typically requires a credit score of at least 620.

Debt consolidation loan—A type of mortgage product that enables a person, by refinancing his or her mortgage, to obtain cash to pay off outstanding higher-interest debt. A debt consolidation loan can be part of a new mortgage or a separate loan using home equity as collateral.

Deed—A written document indicating that a described property is being transferred from the current owner (grantor) to a new owner (grantee).

Deed of trust—A security instrument used in some states, similar to a mortgage, that is recorded in public records, involves three parties—the person borrowing (trustor), the lender (beneficiary), and a neutral third party (trustee) who holds temporary and partial title to the property—summarizes the legal rights of both lender and borrower (including the ability of the lender to foreclose on the property if the loan goes into default), and is canceled when the debt is paid.

Equity—The percentage of the value of a home that the owner actually owns, as distinct from the percentage owed to the lender (through a mortgage, for example).

Fannie Mae—Federal National Mortgage Association (FNMA), a federally chartered enterprise owned by private stockholders that purchases residential mortgages from lenders (thereby providing funds for new loans) and converts them into securities for sale to investors.

Fixed-rate mortgage–A common type of mortgage product for which the interest rate and all monthly payments remain the same throughout the life of the loan, typically 15, 20, or 30 years.

Freddie Mac—Federal Home Loan Mortgage Corporation (FHLMC), a federally chartered corporation that purchases residential mortgages from lenders (thereby providing funds for new loans) and converts them into securities for sale to investors.

Ginnie Mae—Government National Mortgage Association (GNMA), a government-owned corporation established within the U.S. Department of Housing and Urban Development (HUD) to promote nationwide access to mortgage credit by pooling FHA-insured and VA-guaranteed loans in order to back securities for private investment.

Good-faith estimate—An estimate of all closing fees, including prepaid and escrow items and lender charges, that the lender or mortgage broker must provide to the borrower within three days after he or she applies for a loan.

Home Equity Line of Credit (HELOC)—A type of second mortgage that provides the borrower with a firm commitment from the lender to make a specified amount of funds available for a specified period of time, using the equity in the borrower's home as collateral. During the term of the loan agreement, the borrower can borrow any amount of money up to the credit limit at any time and as often as he or she wants and pay back the outstanding balance over time. The interest rate is adjustable and the interest is calculated daily. A HELOC has an annual fee. This type of loan can be used as a financial safety net that a homeowner taps only when and if it's needed.

Home equity loan—A type of second mortgage that provides the borrower one lump sum of money that he or she must pay back over a specified period of time at a fixed interest rate, using his or her home as collateral. As with a fixed-rate mortgage, the monthly payment on a home equity loan remains constant. Interest rates for home equity loans are typically higher than for mortgages, but lower than for other types of loans, such as credit cards or car loans. The home equity loan has tax benefits, but they're more limited than with a mortgage: Typically, borrowers can deduct interest on home equity loans up to only $100,000. One of the big benefits to this type of loan is that the money can be used for almost anything.

Home inspector—A person experienced, qualified, and often licensed to perform an independent inspection of a home, typically at the buyer's request and expense, to find any major problems before the purchase takes place.

HUD-1 Settlement Statement—A document prepared by the closing agent that details all of the information relating to the sale of the home, including price, amount of financing, loan fees, loan-related charges, real estate taxes due, and amounts to be paid by the seller and the buyer. All of the information on the HUD-1 should correspond to details in the *good faith estimate* and *truth-in-lending statement.* At the closing, both the seller and the buyer sign this document; the lender keeps the original.

Interest rate—In relation to a mortgage, the amount of interest charged on a monthly loan payment, usually expressed as a percentage.

Lender—The party that funds the mortgage and to whom the borrower owes the money—a bank, a credit union, a mortgage company, an investor, or even the U.S. government.

Letter of commitment—A document from the mortgage broker or lender stating that an applicant has been approved for a mortgage, the amount of the loan, and the terms.

Loan officer—The employee of the mortgage broker who is a borrower's primary contact throughout the application, approval, and closing process. Also known as a *mortgage consultant* or a *broker associate,* this person will often work on a commission basis, based on the mortgage products he or she sells.

Loan-to-value (LTV)—The ratio between the value of the property and the amount of the loan. For example, a 20-percent down payment means an LTV of 80 percent and a five-percent down payment means an LTV of 95 percent. Many types of mortgages have a specific LTV as a requirement for approval.

Lock/lock-in—An agreement in which the lender guarantees a specified interest rate on a mortgage for a certain length of time at a certain cost. A rate lock is not a loan approval.

Mortgage—A security instrument used in most states, similar to a deed of trust, that creates a lien on the property that is recorded in public records, involves two parties—the person borrowing (mortgagor) and the lender (mortgagee)—and gives the mortgagor full title to the property and gives the lender the right to sell the secured property if the mortgagor defaults (a sales process called foreclosure).

Mortgage banker—A company that makes home loans using its own money and then sells the mortgages to secondary mortgage lenders such as Fannie Mae or Freddie Mac or investors such as insurance companies.

Mortgage broker—An intermediary between a borrower and a lender. Most mortgage brokers represent multiple lenders and typically offer a broader range of mortgage products than a traditional bank. Mortgage brokers earn a fee for the services they provide. Over 80 percent of home buyers in the U.S. work through a mortgage broker.

Mortgage consultant—The person who works for the mortgage broker who is a borrower's primary contact throughout the application, approval, and closing process. Also known as a *broker associate* or a *loan officer*, this person will often work on a commission basis, based on the mortgage products he or she sells.

Mortgage note—The formal written and legally binding agreement between the home buyer and the lender that states the terms of the loan, includes the buyer's promise to repay the debt, and specifies penalties that could be imposed if payments are late or skipped.

Mortgage preapproval—A commitment from a lender to an applicant for a mortgage, after an in-depth process, assuming that all of the borrower's qualifications remain intact at the time of the purchase and allowing for negation of the preapproval in case of a sudden increase in debt, drop in income, or drop in a credit score.

Mortgage prequalification—An estimate of the size of the mortgage for which an applicant could qualify that a mortgage broker or lender provides based on the applicant's credit history, credit score, debt, and income. The prequalification process is not binding and does not require the borrower to provide any formal financial documentation or complete a detailed application.

Offer—A formal, written bid to buy that includes the address of the home, the bid, the type of financing to be used, and a target date for closing and occupancy. It should list contingencies that must be met for the offer to be binding. It may be accompanied by a deposit, which may or may not be refundable, depending on the situation. The offer should be made through a real estate agent, although it can be made independently.

Point—A fee the borrower pays to the lender or broker, one percent of the loan amount before the end of the term. This is used by the lender as an incentive against refinancing.

Preapproval—See *Mortgage preapproval*.

Prepayment penalty—A fee that a lender can charge the borrower for paying off the loan

Prequalification—See *Mortgage prequalification*.

Prime rate—The interest rate at which commercial financial institutions make short-term loans to borrowers whose credit is so good that there is little risk to the lender. This rate fluctuates based on economic conditions and may differ among financial institutions. The prime rate serves as a basis for the interest rates charged for other loans for which the risk is higher.

Principal—The amount of money borrowed, not including interest, taxes, or insurance premiums associated with the mortgage.

Private mortgage insurance (MPI)—Policy typically required by lenders of borrowers applying for a conventional mortgage but unable to pay 20 percent down, which guarantees the lender will be paid even if the borrower defaults on the loan. The lower the down payment, the higher the cost of this insurance, which is added to the monthly payment. Once the borrower owns at least 20-percent equity in the home, this insurance can be canceled and the mortgage can be adjusted accordingly.

Purchase and sale agreement—A written and legally binding contract that both the buyer and the seller sign, outlining the terms, conditions, contingencies, and timetable for the sale of a property and describing the rights of the buyer and the seller pertaining to the transaction.

Real estate agent—A person who is licensed in a specific state to negotiate and arrange for the sale of real estate.

Realtor®—A licensed real estate agent who is a member of the National Association of Realtors®.

Refinance (aka refi)—The process by which a mortgagor pays off a loan with the proceeds from a new loan, typically using the same property as security for the new loan. The goal is typically to obtain a lower interest rate, reduce the monthly payment, shorten the duration of the loan, or cash out some of the equity.

Rescission period—Three full days after receiving all required disclosures and signing loan documents in which a borrower is allowed to cancel a refinance mortgage. Federal law allows this cancellation (rescission) period for certain loan transactions secured by the borrower's home, but not for loans made to purchase, construct, or acquire a primary residence or for transactions secured by a secondary residence or rental property

Second mortgage—A loan a homeowner can obtain in addition to his or her primary mortgage. Just as with a primary mortgage, the home is used as collateral. This second mortgage is totally separate from the first mortgage, with its own rate and terms. The lender for the second mortgage is not entitled to any proceeds from the sale of the home until the lender on the first mortgage has been repaid. Because the risk of default is greater, rates for second mortgages tend to be higher than for first mortgages.

Sub-prime borrower—A person who doesn't meet the approval guidelines for a prime rate mortgage, due to a below-average credit score, a negative credit history, lack of employment information, the inability to provide various financial documents or verifiable income, or even a bankruptcy.

Sub-prime lender —A lender or mortgage broker specializing in working with sub-prime borrowers and that offering a range of home financing options with less strict or nontraditional approval guidelines.

Truth-in-lending statement (TIL)—A document provided by a lender to a mortgage applicant that details information about the mortgage, including the estimated monthly payment and all of the costs associated with the loan, including finance charges. If any of these figures change prior to the closing, the lender will revise the TIL and provide the update to the buyer at the closing.

Index